The Ugly Truth About the Anti-Defamation League

by the Editors of Executive Intelligence Review

The Ugly Truth About the Anti-Defamation League

by the Editors of
Executive Intelligence Review

Executive Intelligence Review
Washington, D.C.
1992

ISBN 0-943235-07-3
Copyright © 1992
Library of Congress Catalogue Number: 92-075810
Printed in the U.S.A.
For information contact the publisher:
Executive Intelligence Review
P.O. Box 17390
Washington, D.C. 20041-0390
EIB 92-006
$7.00

Contents

Since the First Printing: ADL in Middle of A Spy Scandal Too Big to Bury

On January 15, eight days after the publication of the first edition of this book, *The San Francisco Chronicle* shocked the public with the revelation that the office of the ADL in San Francisco was at the center of a scandal involving a San Francisco police officer and a Bay Area art dealer/self-described private eye who were suspected of selling illegally obtained information to agents of the South African government.

The two men, Sgt. Tom Gerard of the San Francisco Police Department, and Roy Bullock, a longtime paid undercover operative for the local office of the Anti-Defamation League of B'nai B'rith (ADL), had been under Federal Bureau of Investigation (FBI) scrutiny since

1990, when federal agents discovered that secret Bureau records on American black Muslims had been obtained by South African spies.

The trail pointed to Bullock, who, in addition to his fulltime paid work for the ADL, had been "moonlighting" as an undercover snitch for the Bureau. On at least one occasion, Bullock received a $500 cash payment from the FBI for infiltrating meetings of two Bay Area groups.

Bullock had access to confidential Bureau files, and became a suspect when FBI files showed up in the hands of the South African government at the same time he was regularly meeting with two South African spies and passing confidential data to them. Bullock received cash payments that eventually totaled over $16,000.

The early meetings between Bullock and the two South African agents, identified as "Humphries" and "Louie,' included policeman Gerard. Later, Bullock would meet with the South Africans alone. According to one version of the Bullock-South Africa story, it was ADL officials who put him in touch with the foreign agents.

Nearly three years later, that FBI probe of South African spying has mushroomed into one of the biggest espionage scandals in years. And the center of the scandal has shifted from cops and art dealers to an alleged command center. The central target is now the ADL.

On April 1, 1993, San Francisco Assistant District Attorney John Dwyer told reporters: "The ADL is the target. Their involvement is just so great. People have called this the Gerard case. Now, it's the ADL case. Gerard is just their guy in San Francisco. The ADL is doing the same thing all over the country. There is evidence that the ADL had police agents in other cities. The case just gets bigger every day. The more we look, the more we find people involved."

The San Francisco probe soon proved that the profile of the ADL contained in this book is right on the
mark.

Far from living up to its thoroughly undeserved and
self-promoted reputation, the Anti-Defamation League
has been caught by San Francisco police investigators:

● illegally spying on at least 950 political organiza-
tions, including the National Association for the Ad-
vancement of Colored People (NAACP), the Rainbow
Coalition, Greenpeace, the Simon Wiesenthal Center, the
United Auto Workers, the Christic Institute, New Jewish
Agenda, Operation Rescue, the Liberty Lobby, the Nation
of Islam, the United Farm Workers, Act-Up, the American
Civil Liberties Union, the National Lawyers Guild, the Bo
Gritz Presidential Campaign and the political movement
led by Lyndon LaRouche;

● infiltrating countless police and sheriff departments across the country, bribing police officers and
illegally obtaining classified government data on at least
20,000 American citizens;

● selling information on anti-apartheid groups to
agents of the South African government;

● passing surveillance and classified police data on
Arab-Americans to Israeli authorities who then used the
ADL data to illegally detain American citizens visiting
Israel;

● passing off Israeli intelligence propaganda as ADL-
generated research in an effort to sway American public
opinion and government policy, while never being
forced to register as foreign agents and while even enjoying tax exempt status with the Internal Revenue Service (IRS).

A Nationwide Operation

The San Francisco district attorney and police investigators have concluded that the pattern of illegal spying that they unearthed in California is a small part of a nationwide spy operation run centrally out of the ADL's national headquarters in New York City under the direction of its "fact finding" director Irwin Suall.

In the San Francisco probe alone, police uncovered evidence that the ADL had illegally penetrated 20 different police agencies in California alone, and had also gained access to classified police files in Chicago, St. Louis, Atlanta, and a half dozen other cities across the country.

On April 8, 1993, San Francisco police released nearly 800 pages of documents, providing previously classified details of the ADL's nationwide criminal operations. Those documents were released as attachments to a search warrant affidavit which police executed the same day. In raids on the San Francisco and Los Angeles offices of the ADL, police obtained "a mountain" of new evidence of the spying and agent-provocateur operations of the League.

The April 8 search warrant actions, which garnered financial records and internal ADL correspondence between Suall and West Coast regional ADL officials, were the second raids on ADL offices in four months. On Dec. 10, 1992, San Francisco police raided the San Francisco and Los Angeles ADL offices, as well as the residences of Bullock and Gerard.

Damage Control Fails

Shortly after the April raids and document disclosures, the ADL launched what local San Francisco newspapers labeled a massive "damage control" effort. They sent out several delegations of national officials from New York and Washington, D.C. to try to derail the probe. Leading the delegations were: ADL National Chairman Melvin Salberg, ADL Executive Director Abraham Foxman and ADL General Counsel Barbara Wahl of the Washington, D.C. law firm of Arent Fox.

In San Francisco, Richard Goldman, the city's chief of protocol and a longtime ADL ally, was caught armtwisting Chief of Police Tony Ribera into bringing the investigation to a halt. Although the city's Police Commission did bend to the ADL pressure and dropped its own probe of the League's interference in local police operations, district attorney Arlo Smith vowed to continue his criminal investigation despite the pressure, and subsequently identified the ADL's national fact-finding director Suall as a prime target.

In behind-closed-doors meetings with publishers, editors, and reporters from *The Los Angeles Times,* the ADL tried to silence the press through cajoling, armtwisting and not-so-subtle allegations of anti-Semitism.

But the ADL-run Jewish weekly, *Heritage Southwest Jewish Press,* more openly expressed the ADL's true feelings about the probe. Publisher Herb Brin, just returned from a trip to Belgrade, Serbia where he gave his unabashed editorial endorsement to the Serbian slaughter of Bosnian Moslems and Croats, wrote on April 16:

"Lyndon LaRouche, from his federal prison cell, must be gloating. . . . Calypso Gene Farrakhan is singing away at the chagrin of ADL. These—among a host of skinheads, pinkos and nuts—are dancing because San Francisco cops are on a vicious hunt to embarrass the Anti-Defamation League for doing what ADL has always done and must do to serve mankind—after Hitler.

"And the bastard decision by some idiotic editors of *The Los Angeles Times* to play into the game—and

Heritage will find out what prompted the malicious hunt into the fact-finding efforts of ADL (better believe it!)— speaks for itself as *The Times* played the trumped-up 'ADL investigated' story on Page One on 'Good Friday'. . . . Hardly a week passes that I don't supply Jewish defense material to David Lehrer, head of ADL in this region . . . A people must have the will and moxy to defend themselves—and that, to me, is what ADL is all about. . . . The San Francisco police charge that ADL maintains political intelligence operations in some seven U.S. cities. In which case I say: Hooray for ADL!"

Brin, a promoter of the terrorist Jewish Defense League, and gutter-level ADL snitch for 40 years, was openly threatening revenge. Soon after Brin's diatribe, some local news outlets experienced nastier treatment than the name-calling directed against *The Los Angeles Times*. KPOO-FM, a local black community radio station in the Bay Area, began receiving threatening calls after they aired a series of interviews with victims of ADL spying. "Jew-hating nigger," "nigger Nazi," and other similar epithets bombarded the station's phone lines.

In the past, these kinds of ADL hooligan tactics never failed to work. This time, however, the sheer weight of evidence has made this one scandal too big to bury.

By late April, after police publicly released the inventory of documents seized from the ADL, the League's fact-finding director Irwin Suall hired a top criminal defense lawyer in San Francisco, the clearest signal yet that the ADL is shaking over the idea that at long last, they have been caught in the act of being themselves.

Spying on Jews

David Gurvitz was unhappy about his pay from the ADL. As the League's chief fact-finder in their Los Angeles office, the 35-year-old Gurvitz was married, with one child and a second one on the way. His fulltime job at the ADL paid him slightly more than $20,000 a year, hardly enough to live on in a high-cost town like LA. So, in June 1992, Gurvitz went to the Los Angeles Simon Wiesenthal Center, another Jewish group involved in monitoring the activities of so-called hate groups, to ask them for a better-paying job.

But unfortunately the Wiesenthal Center already had a fulltime staff researcher, Rick Eaton, and Gurvitz was given the brushoff by Wiesenthal Center director Rabbi Cooper.

Gurvitz's response to the job rejection was typical ADL. He staked out the Wiesenthal Center to get Eaton's car license plate number and passed the plate number to his ADL counterpart in San Francisco, Roy Bullock. Gurvitz would later tell San Francisco police and FBI investigators that Bullock was his "mentor."

Bullock contacted Sgt. Tom Gerard and had Gerard get Eaton's California Department of Motor Vehicles records.

The State of California has very strict laws prohibiting private citizens from possessing DMV records. Those records contain photographs, addresses, Social Security numbers, fingerprints, and other sensitive personal data. Unauthorized possession of even one DMV record is a felony punishable by a stiff fine and a five-year term in a California state prison. When Gurvitz got Bullock and Gerard to obtain Eaton's DMV record, all three were committing a serious state crime.

But when police raided the home/office of Roy Bullock on Dec. 10 last year, they found far more than the Eaton records. They found DMV records on more than 1,300 Californians in a computer spy base which included data on 12,000 individuals and 950 political groups.

Among the files in the Bullock computer were the DMV records of nearly one-third of the membership of the Arab-American Anti-Discrimination Committee (AADC), a nationwide Arab-American organization involved in legitimate political activities. For years, leaders and offices of the AADC had been the targets of threats of violence.

In 1985, Jewish Defense League (JDL) terrorists carried out bomb attacks against AADC offices in Santa Ana, California, Washington, D.C., and Boston, Massachusetts. In the Santa Ana attack, regional director Alex Odeh was killed. ADL agent Bullock has admitted to police interviewers that he had infiltrated the AADC and personally had a key to its Santa Ana office at the time of the Odeh murder.

ADL-BATF Collusion

The Gurvitz-Bullock efforts against Eaton did not stop with the illegal spying. Next, to intimidate Eaton, Gurvitz asked Bullock to contact a leading member of the White Aryan Resistance (WAR), a West Coast-based white supremacist organization. The WAR leader, whose ADL codename was "Scumbag," is a convicted felon, and an undercover agent provocateur on the payroll of the ADL and the Treasury Department's Bureau of Alcohol, Tobacco and Firearms (BATF). "Scumbag" had been regularly meeting with Bullock and San Francisco BATF agents, providing inside information about WAR. Through this channel, Bullock and the ADL apparently maintained wiretaps on the WAR phone, codenaming the effort "Operation Eavesdrop."

(The case of "Scumbag" opens the question of another level of criminal activity—receipt of federal confidential records. BATF had offered to "share" the infiltrator "Scumbag" if the ADL would pay informant fees—some several hundred dollars a week. The money for "Scumbag" was approved by the ADL's chief fact-finder, Irwin Suall, from the League's national headquarters in New York City.)

So, when in the fall of 1992, Bullock contacted "Scumbag" and gave him details about Rick Eaton's efforts to infiltrate and spy on WAR, it was a textbook dirty trick. Bullock hoped to enhance "Scumbag's" position within the WAR group by having him expose the infiltrator, Eaton. The ADL would gain greater hands-on control over the group, through its own informant. Bullock also hoped that WAR might take some kind of action against Eaton that would scare him into leaving his job with the Wiesenthal Center—opening the position for Gurvitz.

There was only one problem. Apparently unbeknownst to Bullock, the FBI was tapping his phone as part of the South Africa espionage probe. His conversations with Gerard, Gurvitz, and "Scumbag" were all recorded.

The FBI had no choice but to warn Eaton at the Wiesenthal Center about a possible physical attack against him by WAR. According to documents released by the San Francisco police, the FBI could not rule out an actual assassination attempt against Eaton.

FBI agents also went to the Los Angeles ADL office in October 1992 to alert them to the Gurvitz-Bullock dirty trick. The ADL response was striking. Gurvitz was fired on the spot, despite his family financial problems and pregnant wife. Only employed by the ADL for four years, Gurvitz was expendable.

Bullock, however, a 40-year employee of the ADL,

was too valuable to fire. At that very moment, Bullock (just caught running a possible assassination through White Aryan Resistance) was in Germany as part of a high-level ADL delegation meeting with government officials and top German law enforcement to peddle their credentials as "experts" on extremist groups. Bullock personally met with the head of the German Constitutional Protection Office (BfV), Germany's equivalent of the FBI, to receive and pass on information about U.S. skinhead and neo-Nazi activities. Needless to say, Bullock did not report on his own role in running agents provocateurs inside those circles.

When Bullock did return to San Francisco and the prospect of being dumped for his antics with WAR, he did not lose his job. Irwin Suall, the chief dirty-trickster for the ADL; his Washington, D.C. aide, Mira Lansky Boland; David Lehrer, the head of the ADL's Los Angeles office; and Rick Hirschhaut, the league's San Francisco director, all threatened to quit on the spot if any action were taken against Bullock. Suall even wrote a memo which police uncovered in their searches of the San Francisco ADL office, lauding Bullock as the ADL's "number one investigator."

The impromptu rally in support of Bullock by top ADL officials speaks volumes about the real nature of the ADL. Bullock's dirty tricks with WAR were not restricted to the targeting of Eaton. Bullock regularly tried to recruit white supremacists, KKKers, and others from the radical racist right to join AADC and other Arab-American groups, in order to later "expose" those groups for their alleged anti-Semitic ties.

Eaton wasn't the only Jewish activist targetted by the ADL. Stewart Alpert, a national leader of the New Jewish Agenda, and other members of the group were

ADL targets. Vera Katz, the mayor of Portland, Oregon, who lived for years on a kibbutz in Israel, discovered that her sister city program was spied upon by the ADL.

A Dilemma for the FBI

Shortly after the Eaton affair, the FBI asked the San Francisco Police to take charge of the probe of Bullock and Gerard. Once the investigation had turned into a probe of the ADL, the Bureau ran up against a very embarrassing dilemma.

Most serious was the record of FBI collusion with the ADL. On Feb. 4, 1985, then FBI Director William Webster wrote a priority cable to the special agents in charge of the FBI's 25 largest field offices, ordering them to establish permanent local liaison to the ADL. The Webster order coincided with a major effort by the ADL to solicit a federal prosecution of Lyndon LaRouche, a longstanding target of ADL spying and dirty tricks.

Ironically, this FBI order came precisely when the "Jewish underground," which FBI Director Webster later identified as the number-one terrorist threat in the United States, was on a terrorist spree that covered New York, New Jersey, and California. Terrorist activities had left two people dead, including Alex Odeh, the Arab-American leader.

By Dec. 10, 1986, documents obtained under the Freedom of Information Act (FOIA) show ADL National Director Nathan Perlmutter, writing to Webster, to work details for the ADL to give annual training lectures at the FBI Academy in Quantico, Va. on "hate crimes."

On Nov. 21, 1989, Thomas F. Jones, deputy assistant director of the FBI in charge of the criminal investigations division wrote to Irwin Suall to invite Suall and his

ADL associates, Allan Schwartz and Michael Lieberman, to lecture the top 50 FBI agents on "civil rights law."

The marriage between the FBI and the ADL since February 1985 raises serious questions of legality. Was the ADL handed authority to run a revised "parallel COINTELPRO program" after the U.S. Congress had essentially outlawed the FBI's spying on non-criminal political groups in 1975? The ADL's intimate ties to the Treasury Department's BATF ring similar alarm bells. When the San Francisco ADL office was caught in possession of dozens of police intelligence reports on "skinheads" prepared by the Portland police, ADL Northwest Regional Director Marvin Stern told reporter Phil Stanford that perhaps the files show ADL's "work for the government."

Under the Reagan administration's Executive Order 12333, which spelled out guidelines for domestic and foreign spying, the FBI was given broad latitude to use non-government personnel as "assets."

No wonder the FBI dropped the probe of Bullock-Gerard on the grounds that it might jeopardize FBI secrets, methods, and procedures!

Local Probe, National Target

With the Bullock-Gerard case in its hands, the San Francisco police launched an ambitious investigation late last year under the supervision of Captain John Willett, head of the Special Investigations Division.

In November 1992, shortly after being interviewed by the FBI, Tom Gerard fled to the Philippines, which has no extradition treaty with the United States. From his retreat on a remote Filipino island, Gerard formally submitted his resignation from the SFPD. Ironically, Gerard's last assignment was in the SID offices.

On Jan. 22, 1993, Gerard told *The San Francisco Examiner* (from the Phillipines) that he had first met Bullock at the San Francisco ADL office in 1985: "We sat there one morning with everyone in the (ADL) office, shook hands and made friends." Gerard freely admitted he funnelled classified police data to Bullock with the full understanding that it was for the ADL. "The guy (Bullock) had no criminal record. It's like we're talking to someone in the neighborhood community watch organization."

Gerard had just returned to the San Francisco Police Department after a two-year leave of absence in which he worked for the CIA, ostensibly as a bomb expert. According to documents and interviews, Gerard's CIA assignments included El Salvador, Afghanistan, and a covert operation targeted at the African nation of Ghana. On his return to the police department, Gerard frequently boasted to his colleagues that he was also working closely with the Israeli Mossad. In retrospect, the references to Mossad may have been based on his budding relationship with the ADL.

Gerard's work for the ADL did not go unrewarded.

In May 1991, Gerard was one of eleven police officers from across the country who traveled to Israel on an all-expenses-paid ADL junket. The group's escort was Mira Lansky Boland, the ADL's Washington, D.C. factfinder who personally put the delegation together. Sgt. Tim Carroll, a detective with the San Diego County Sheriff's Department, described the journey as a payment for services already rendered to the ADL. "A lot of it was for past work or relationship with the ADL and kind of an emotional thing that we spread the word when we get back. . . ."

Police officers from Boston, Washington, Mobile,

Dallas, Maryland, Virginia, and Georgia also went along on the junket, which featured meetings with senior Israeli police, military, and intelligence officials.

One junket participant, Donald Moore, was subsequently indicted on kidnapping conspiracy charges, when, on behalf of the Cult Awareness Network (CAN), he joined in a plot to kidnap a du Pont family heir, Lewis du Pont Smith, a close associate of Lyndon LaRouche. When Moore was arraigned in late September 1992, his attorney, Mark Rasch, was from the ADL's law firm. Mira Lansky Boland was in court throughout most of the trial.

In taped conversations with the FBI's undercover informant inside the kidnap conspiracy, Moore boasted that he had worked closely with the ADL against LaRouche and that as a deputy sheriff in Loudoun County, Va. he had conducted illegal wiretaps, breakins and other crimes against the LaRouche group. Though Moore was acquitted, his codefendant, Galen Kelly, was convicted of federal kidnapping charges in May 1993.

FBI Files on Nation of Islam

The hostess of the May 1991 Israel trip, Mira Lansky Boland, may face criminal charges for illegal possession of a classified FBI intelligence report on the Nation of Islam (NOI), a legitimate political group. The ADL's Gurvitz told FBI and SFPD investigators that he personally sent copies of the FBI document to Boland after he retrieved it from the ADL's Los Angeles office files.

Lansky Boland had put out a request to all ADL offices for information on the Nation of Islam, as part of an ADL propaganda drive against the group. The FBI internal criminal investigation report, a 35-page document prepared some time in the late 1980s, was leaked to the ADL after the FBI apparently closed the probe without indicting anyone in the NOI. But the ADL used the classified report to block the NOI's activities, especially the Dopebusters program, which had successfully bid for contracts to provide security for public housing authorities across the country.

Bullock may have passed the NOI file on to his South African spy friends.

Lansky Boland could also emerge as a pivotal figure in a renewed probe of the Jonathan Jay Pollard spy scandal. A graduate school classmate of Pollard's at a special national security studies program at the Fletcher School of Diplomacy, Lansky Boland was placed in a job with the CIA at the same time Pollard went to work for a Naval Intelligence unit. Both Pollard and Lansky Boland were protégés of the Fletcher program director, Dr. Uri Ra'anan. Ra'anan was a former Israeli intelligence officer who in the 1960s set up an Israeli spy unit at the national headquarters of B'nai B'rith, the parent organization of the ADL.

Pollard, according to a story published in the May 11, 1993 *Village Voice,* has written to friends that a top official of the ADL played a central role in his espionage activities for Israel (and the Soviet Union).

Inside the ADL Files

In April 1992, following the second search of ADL offices, the San Francisco police released some of the spy documents to the public.

The inventory included a computerized list of groups, with the data base broken down into five categories: "pinko," "right," "ANC" (for African National Congress, a South African group that Bullock was spying on for the South African government and the ADL), "Arab" and "skinhead."

Since the ADL had long paraded itself as the antidote to right-wing extremist and "hate groups," it was a shocking revelation for many long-duped collaborators of ADL that the majority of the 950 groups under ADL surveillance were left-wing, liberal, ethnic, human rights, gay, and labor groups. Leading members of the U.S. Congress including Ron Dellums, Paul McCloskey, and Nancy Pelozi, as well as Sen. Allan Cranston, had been spied on by the ADL, according to files seized by the police.

African National Congress leader Chris Hani, who was assassinated in April 1993, was a target of ADL surveillance during several trips to California.

The Christic Institute, which filed a spring 1986 lawsuit against Oliver North, Richard Secord, and others involved in the then-unknown Iran-Contra operations, was surveilled and infiltrated by the ADL. Roy Bullock stole trash from Christic's San Francisco offices and filed detailed reports with the San Francisco ADL, listing bank accounts, personnel data and other sensitive information.

Chip Berlet and Russ Belant, two left-wing "researchers" who worked closely with the ADL for years in efforts to foist Justice Department frameups of LaRouche and his associates, were reportedly shocked when, in a 1986 meeting at ADL headquarters with Irwin Suall, they were told the ADL had detailed files on them. However, from 1986 till as late as 1991, Berlet continued to closely collaborate with the ADL.

Henry Schwartzchild, a former ADL employee, confirmed to *San Francisco Weekly* that the ADL had spied on Rev. Martin Luther King, Jr. "They thought King was sort of a loose cannon. He was a Baptist preacher and nobody could be quite sure what he would do next. The ADL was very anxious about having an unguided missile out there." The NAACP was another prime target of ADL espionage and disruption.

Wilbert Tatum, publisher of New York City's *Amsterdam News,* captured the sense of betrayal in the black community in the first of a series of front-page editorials on the San Francisco spy case on April 24: "There can be no question that the shocking allegation that the Anti-Defamation League has been spying for years on organizations such as the NAACP, New Alliance Party, Ku Klux Klan, Greenpeace, the Arab-American Anti-Discrimination Committee, the Black United Fund, Operation Rescue, the board of directors of public television station KQUE, the San Francisco Bay Guardian newspaper, at least 12,000 individuals nationwide, and still counting, as well as organizations and individuals yet to be named in New York and the East Coast, leaves us numbed and chilled. . . .

"For while it was serving as a model, by all accounts available to us, it was spying on organizations that it was ostensibly helping. Organizations such as the NAACP welcomed this help. . . . They were welcomed into our organizations and into our lives. It is unthinkable to suggest that these 'friends' have betrayed us, as well as so many more. Yet, the investigations by competent authorities in Los Angeles and San Francisco suggest that they have done precisely that, up to and including selling illegally gathered information on organizations and individuals to the apartheid government of South Africa."

San Francisco Assistant District Attorney John Dwyer also revealed that Arab-Americans were not only being spied upon by the ADL. At a court hearing in February, he revealed that one Arab-American whose name appeared in Bullock's computer dossiers had been arrested by Israeli police. The man, Mohammed Jarad, a Chicago grocer, was detained when he arrived in Israel to visit relatives on Jan. 25, 1993. He was held for days before the American embassy was even informed of his arrest.

The DA's office later acknowledged that authorities found foreign government (believed to be from Israel) files on Americans. One Bay Area Middle East peace activist, Jeffery Blankfort, was tracked in the foreign government files throughout an entire tour of the Middle East and North Africa.

A New York City ADL agent, Yehudit Barsky, who worked directly under Suall, regularly received Israeli police dossiers on Arab activists from the Israeli embassy, according to former American Israel Public Affairs Committee (AIPAC) researcher Gregory Slabodkin.

In February, when Israeli Prime Minister Yitzak Rabin came to Washington for the first official meeting with President Clinton, Israeli Defense Force officials admitted that they planted intelligence data in the ADL, which the ADL would then release as its "research."

In Chicago, the ADL's regular spy routine against Arab-Americans, according to writer Robert Friedman, was to conduct video-surveillance of funerals of Chicago-area Arabs, and then give the videos to the Israeli government. Arab-Americans visiting relatives in Israel and the Israeli occupied territories would be taken into Israeli custody and shown the videos as an intimidation tactic.

The Money Trail

In interviews with both the FBI and the San Francisco police, Roy Bullock freely admitted that he was a full-time employee for the ADL. He received $550 a week plus expenses, he had a desk at the ADL's San Francisco office, and was one of only three people with access to the secret files maintained at the ADL's office.

Yet, when police reviewed ADL financial records seized in the Dec. 10 raids, there was no mention of Bullock as an ADL employee. California tax filings also showed no mention of Bullock.

Police eventually uncovered a paper trail involving a prominent Los Angeles tax lawyer, political fixer, and ADL official who systematically concealed Bullock's ties to the ADL.

The attorney, Bruce Hochman, was for years the regional president, and is still today national vice president of the ADL. Hochman admitted to San Francisco police investigators that, beginning in 1960, he would receive checks from the ADL, deposit them in an account and issue cashiers checks to Bullock. The scheme enabled the ADL to avoid payroll taxes, workmen's compensation and other pay-outs. This scheme's illegality should have been obvious to Hochman, who is one of the West Coast's leading tax attorneys. Hochman is also one of an elite among California lawyers which handpicks nominees for federal judgeships.

One of Hochman's proteges, federal immigration Judge Bruce J. Einhorn, who chairs the Los Angeles ADL civil rights committee, is currently at the center of a controversy stemming from his refusal to recuse himself from the "Los Angeles 8" case, involving seven Palestinians and a Kenyan who are being charged with membership in an Arab terrorist group and are targeted for deportation. Back in 1987, when the eight were first arrested, ADL Regional Director David Lehrer publicly boasted that the case was based on data provided to the FBI by the ADL. Today, however, ADL computer spy files naming these 8 defendants open a new scandal about Einhorn's bias.

Although San Francisco investigators say that Hochman is not a target of their probe, evidence was released showing over $160,000 in payments by Hochman to Bullock in recent years. San Francisco D.A. Arlo Smith told reporters that the ADL could be prosecuted on 48 separate felony counts simply for their illegal financial transactions with Bullock.

Money for the ADL's covert "fact-finding" on the West Coast was handled through a covert bank account maintained in the name "L. Patterson" at several Los Angeles banks. Those accounts were maintained by regional director David Lehrer. All of the money was initially provided by the ADL national headquarters in New York, according to San Francisco investigators. The money trail established through documents seized in the December and April raids has prompted investigators to conclude that the league's dirty tricks operations nationwide are micro-managed from ADL headquarters by Suall and his chief deputies, including Lansky Boland.

Civil Suits Pending

San Francisco prosecutors have already handed down one indictment in the ongoing ADL spy probe. On May 6, Tom Gerard returned to San Francisco from his Philippines hide-out and was immediately arrested and charged with five California state felonies. Now released on $20,000 bond, Gerard has been told by prosecutors that he can avoid a jail sentence if he agrees to cooperate. Prosecutors described Gerard and even Bullock as mere "cogs" in the ADL spy machinery. "Look at the top, at the organizational setup, at the fact finders," a source inside the investigation told *The San Francisco Examiner* on May 11.

District Attorney Smith has said the remaining indictments will be handed down by June 15.

In the meantime, the ADL has also been served with a class action lawsuit in California state court by a group of Californians, including Yigal Arens, the son of the former Israeli Defense Minister Moshe Arens, and Helen Hooper McCloskey, the wife of the former Congressman. The suit charges the ADL with illegal spying and violations of the civil rights of a class of California citizens targeted because of their political beliefs. Three employees of *Executive Intelligence Review* magazine from California have also joined the suit, which is expected to result in extensive additional disclosures of the ADL's illegal spy activities.

With evidence mounting and criminal charges pending against the ADL for foreign espionage, domestic spying and financial fraud, many are asking: How long will the ADL manage to retain its tax-exempt status with the IRS? To maintain tax-exempt status a group cannot engage in any kind of direct political campaign activity and cannot serve as an agent of a foreign government.

The ADL has been caught doing both.

In police interviews, David Gurvitz revealed that the ADL ran an army of undercover agents across the country. In Chicago, the ADL had undercover informants code-named "Chi 1-2-3," at least one of whom was a local police officer; in St. Louis, ADL ran "Ironsides;" in Atlanta, an Arab-speaking ADL spy was code-named "Flipper." Elsewhere in California, ADL ran "Scout."

While at first, only the Portland, Oregon district attorney and the Chicago Police Review Board formally announced that they will investigate the ADL spying, as this book goes to print other official government bodies are following the leads.

The ADL Command Structure

National Commission

$

Honorary Chairmen and Vice Chairmen

Kenneth Bialkin

Edgar Bronfman

Philip Klutznick

Sen. Howard
Metzenbaum

Former Sen.
Rudy Boschwitz

Max Kampelman

Rep. Sidney R. Yates

Members

Meyer Eisenberg (Ex. Asst. GC. SEC)
Murray Janus (Richmond, Va.)
Irving Shapiro
Burton Joseph (Minneapolis grain cartel)
Arnold Forster
Justin Finger
Theodore Silbert (Sterling National Bank)

ADL Foundation

ADL staff

Irwin Suall

Mira Lansky Boland
31 regional offices
4 overseas offices

Major Donors

Robert O. Anderson (Atlantic Richfield)

Dwayne Andreas
(ADM)

J. David Barnes (Mellon Bank)
Roger E. Birk (Merrill Lynch)
Edgar Bronfman (Seagrams)
Charles L. Brown (AT&T)
Willard Butcher (Chase Manhattan)
Alvah Chapman (Miami Herald Publishing Co.)
Peter A. Cohen (Shearson American Express)
Lester Crown (Material Services Corp.)
Justin Dart (Dart Industries)
Marvin Davis (20th Century Fox)

Robert Ferguson
(First National
State Bank of
N.J.)

Randolph Hearst (Hearst)
Samuel Higginbottom (Rolls Royce)
Amory Houghton, Jr. (Corning Glass)

Stephen Kay (Goldman Sachs)
Donald Keough (Coca Cola)

Lane Kirkland
(AFL-CIO)

John Kluge (MetroMedia)
Ralph Lazarus (Federated)
John Loeb (Shearson Loeb Rhoades)
J. Willard Marriott (Marriott Corp.)
Paul Miller (First Boston Corp.)
Franklin Murphy (Times Mirror)
Andrall Pearson (Pepsico)
Lester Pollack (United Brands)
Victor Posner (Sharon Steel)
Abram Pritzker (Hyatt)
James D. Robinson (Amex)
Steven Ross (Warner Communications)
William Schreyer (Merrill Lynch)
Arthur Ochs Sulzberger (New York Times)
Alfred Taubman (Taubman Corp.)
S.P. Thomas (Sears Roebuck)
Robert Van Fossan (Mutual Benefit)
Gordon Wallis (Irving Trust)
John Welch (GE)
Walter Wriston (Citibank)

Canon Edward N. West of the Episcopal Cathedral of St. John the Divine in New York City.

Introduction
The Canon Spills
the Beans

It was December 9, 1978. The cold New York City winter was made worse by the damp and spooky setting in which the two undercover investigators found themselves. They were sitting in the cavernous basement study of the Cathedral of St. John the Divine, interviewing Canon Edward West, a senior official of the secretive Sovereign Military and Hospitaller Order of St. John of Jerusalem, Knights of Malta. They had come to ask the Canon about Lyndon LaRouche, the by-then well-known economist and political figure, who had been the recent target of an assassination threat by the Order and some of its agents, including Manhattan District Attorney Robert Morgenthau.

Details of the threat had been published in a thirty-page report issued by LaRouche's associates earlier in the year, and LaRouche's U.S. Labor Party had more recently issued a book-length exposé of the international drug trade, highlighting Britain's role in a new opium war directed against the United States. As a top official of the Protestant Episcopal Church in America, and as a leading Knight of Malta, Canon West was well aware of the LaRouche-commissioned exposés.

After a half-hour of chatter about other subjects, interrupted by a brief photo session memorializing the interview, the investigators brought the discussion around to LaRouche and the potential problems he and his organization posed to the Anglo-American establishment and their secret societies.

The Canon's response to the inquisitive visitors startled them.

In a cold, ruthless tone, the Canon stated confidently: "We will not get directly involved. We will have our Jewish friends at the Anti-Defamation League deal with Mr. LaRouche and his organization."

Canon West's threat proved prophetic. Already, during the summer of 1978, the ADL, in league with the British Fabian Society-sponsored Heritage Foundation, had published a broadside attack against Lyndon LaRouche as an "anti-Semite." The ADL was well aware of LaRouche's efforts beginning in 1975 to bring about a peaceful solution to the Middle East crisis by designing and lobbying internationally for a regional economic development program that would improve the lives of Jews and Arabs alike. LaRouche had traveled to Baghdad, Iraq and had also conferred with senior Israeli government officials about his peace plan. The ADL knew that the characterization of LaRouche as an "anti-Semite" was absurdly libelous.

Nevertheless, the ADL's campaign to smear and eventually destroy LaRouche and his movement escalated dramatically over the winter of 1978-79, and has continued ever since at a cost of tens of millions of dollars.

The bizarre reference to the nominally Jewish civil rights group by Episcopal Canon West, with his pivotal role in the secret British Freemasonic movement in America, naturally prompted a more serious inquiry by LaRouche's associates into the ADL, especially following the sudden burst of ADL venom during the summer of 1978.

What that investigation revealed was as shocking as the initial comments by Canon West about "our Jewish friends." Not only is the ADL emphatically *not* a Jewish civil rights lobby; the ADL, and its parent agency, B'nai B'rith, have been, from their inception, arms of the British secret intelligence agencies and secret societies that are sworn enemies of the United States. The B'nai B'rith and the ADL have used their nominal Jewishness to conceal their actual allegiance and agenda.

The early history of B'nai B'rith is part of one of the ugliest chapters in the British-led Confederate secessionist insurrection against the Union in the 19th century. The ADL is more closely aligned with the racist Ku Klux Klan than with Judaism; more closely aligned with the murderous Medellín Cocaine Cartel than with any civic group. As the financial and political institutions of the United States have fallen deeper and deeper into the grip of illegal drug money, the visibility and power of the ADL has grown. Today, they are at the very center of the corruption of our most cherished institutions: our schools, our courts, and our elected officials.

This little book is by no means a comprehensive profile of the B'nai B'rith and the ADL. Such a serious history would require volumes. It is written in order to give you, the reader, a brief glimpse of the ugly truth about the ADL: They are a bunch of racist thugs who push drugs.

Scottish Rite Freemason and Ku Klux Klan founder Confederate Gen. Albert Pike's statue in Washington, D.C.'s Judiciary Square.

1 150 Years of Perfidy

$\mathbf{A}$pril 14, 1865, the day President Abraham Lincoln was shot, will live forever as a day of infamy for American patriots and lovers of freedom all over the world. But for the leadership of the Order of B'nai B'rith and its 20th-century secret police arm, the Anti-Defamation League, April 14, 1865 is a day that will be long remembered for a very different reason. The B'nai B'rith, a pivotal player in the British Freemasonic plot to destroy the Union, was implicated in Lincoln's assassination! That fact does not square very well with its long-cultivated, but totally unwarranted reputation as a Jewish social service organization and a champion of civil rights. For that reason, B'nai B'rith and the ADL have gone to great lengths to bury that history.

Simon Wolf (1835-1923) was the Washington, D.C.

lawyer for the Order of B'nai B'rith during the entire
period of the U.S. Civil War. He would later head the
International Order of B'nai B'rith for many years. In
1862, Wolf was arrested by LaFayette C. Baker, the chief
of detectives for the city of Washington, D.C., and later
Lincoln's chief of the U.S. Secret Service, on charges that
Wolf was involved in spying and blockade running on
behalf of the Confederacy. Baker arrested Wolf, who was
the attorney representing a number of Jews accused of
spying for the South, on the grounds that he was part of
a "conspiratorial organization" working on behalf of the
secessionist cause behind the lines in the nation's capital.
The conspiratorial organization named by Baker was the
B'nai B'rith!

Both Baker and U.S. Gen. Ulysses S. Grant targeted
the Order of B'nai B'rith as a Confederate spy agency.
Upon taking command of the Western Front in 1862,
General Grant issued Order No. 11, which expelled all
Jews from the military district within 24 hours of its
implementation. U.S. Grant was no anti-Semite. He was
reacting to the activities of B'nai B'rith and leading Confederates like Judah P. Benjamin. Lincoln, however, cog-
nizant of the need to avoid blanket attacks against religious or ethnic groups, rescinded the order.

A 1987 B'nai B'rith authorized biography of Simon
Wolf by Esther L. Panitz offered the following highly
suggestive, albeit incomplete description of Wolf's personal relationship with President Lincoln's assassin, John
Wilkes Booth. Bear in mind that this biography, written
on the basis of B'nai B'rith's archives, paints Wolf in the
most favorable of lights. The mere fact that the author
had to include Wolf's links to Booth, and Wolf's earlier

arrest as an alleged Confederate spy and blockade runner, implies that the actual story is far uglier:

> "Wolf's concern for culture first expressed itself in the
> formation of a private club, devoted to the arts and
> humanities and frequented by young men avid for learn-
> ing. ... Were pride and ambition his only motives in
> seeking the intellectual life? Clearly, Wolf hoped that if he
> and his friends would devote themselves to the pursuit of
> learning, they would deflect the prejudicial statements
> of their Christian neighbors. Wolf was upset that terms
> such as 'money-changers,' 'cotton traders,' and 'clothes
> dealers' had become words of reproach. ...
>
> "Locally, the group's theatrical productions re-
> ceived a good press. Wolf, who would often play the
> Ghost in Hamlet or Shylock in The Merchant of Venice,
> bore an uncanny resemblance to John Wilkes Booth,
> Lincoln's assassin. Earlier in Cleveland, Booth had joined
> Wolf and Peixotto in dramatic performances. Years after-
> ward, Wolf remembered that he had met Booth once
> again at the Willard Hotel, on the morning of the day
> Lincoln was shot. There, at the bar, Booth explained that
> Senator John P. Hale's daughter had just rejected his
> marriage proposal. Wolf attributed Lincoln's murder to
> this personal tragedy in Booth's own life. ... Wolf also
> recalled that once he sat for a picture entitled 'The Assas-
> sination of President Lincoln.' "

In his own book, *Presidents I Have Known,* Wolf
says that he and his longtime acquaintance John Wilkes
Booth did some drinking together at the Willard Hotel
on the day Booth shot Lincoln.

Wolf's, and a second leading B'nai B'rith figure, Benjamin Peixotto's, dealings with John Wilkes Booth were
hardly cultural. Nor could Wolf have possibly believed
that Abraham Lincoln was killed because of John Wilkes

Booth's unrequited love affair. Even John Hinckley, the would-be assassin of President Ronald Reagan, was declared insane when he tried to peddle the line that he had tried to kill Ronald Reagan due to an unfulfilled fantasy love affair with actress Jodie Foster.

To understand the circumstances under which B'nai B'rith's Washington, D.C. leader and one of its founding members were circumstantially tied to the Lincoln assassination conspiracy, and explicitly linked to the secessionist insurrection against the Union, it is necessary to look briefly at the circumstances under which the Order of B'nai B'rith was founded in 1843.

Britain's Reconquest Dream

Following the American Revolution, the British monarchy and its East India Company colonialist apparatus never for a moment abandoned their commitment to reconquer the lost colonies in North America. Although the military effort at reconquest in the War of 1812 failed, other efforts to seed the United States with British agents, some drawn from the ranks of anti-republican Tories who were permitted to retain their citizenship and property in America under the terms of the Treaty of Paris of 1783, were more successful.

In 1801, the Tory faction of U.S. Freemasonry—the grouping of Freemasons who had sided with England during the American Revolution—opened up shop as the "Grand Council of the Princes of Jerusalem of the Mother Supreme Council of the Knights Commander of the House of the Temple of Solomon of the Thirty-third Degree of the Ancient and Accepted Order of the Scottish Rite of Freemasonry in the United States." This U.S.-based British Freemasonic lodge was chartered in

Charleston, S.C. The members of this British-led secret society would direct the Confederate secessionist insurrection a half-century later. Other Scottish Rite members would be among the founders of the B'nai B'rith. They, too, would be leading Confederates.

Apart from the esoteric mission of spreading an explicitly anti-Christian form of Roman pagan worship and occultism among the early generations of American citizens, the Charleston lodge also sought to build up a network of pro-British merchants, spies and politicians in both the North and the South, who would one day play a pivotal role in the reconquest. Many of these early Masons became wealthy through their business dealings with the British East India Company and the Dutch West India Company, in both the cotton and the slave trade.

Among the founding members of the Charleston Scottish Rite Lodge were many prominent Jews, including Isaac DaCosta, Moses Cohen, Israel De Lieben, Dr. Isaac Held, Moses Levi, and Moses Peixotto. Many of these men were Sephardic Jews from North Africa or from Spain who had originally settled in the Caribbean and engaged in the early slave trade. These Jewish Masons set up other organizations which also maintained active liaison to Great Britain's powerful Jewish community. The Hebrew Orphan Aid Society was one such nominally benign group that would produce one of the most rabid secessionist leaders, Judah P. Benjamin.

Although today, any reports of the Freemasonic roots and structure of B'nai B'rith are usually greeted with a torrent of allegations of "anti-Semitism," back in the formative years, B'nai B'rith's own magazine *The Menorah* offered the following information about the founders of the group:

"Their reunions were frequent and several of them being members of existing benevolent societies, especially the order of Free Masons and Odd Fellows, they finally concluded that a somewhat similar organization, but based upon the 'Jewish idea' would best obtain their object. The Jewish religion has many observances and customs corresponding to the secret societies known to us. The synagogue, for instance, might be compared to a lodge room. It used to be open twice a day. For a Jew desiring to find a friend, they had but to go there and make themselves known by a certain sign and token. . . . The sign consisted of a grip with a full hand and the magical word Sholem Alachem. The messussah on the doorpost was the countersign. Shema Israel (Hear, O Israel) was the password."

Indeed, to this day, all local chapters of the B'nai B'rith are referred to as Lodges, a practice borrowed whole cloth from the Scottish Rite.

When Moses saw some Jews of this B'nai B'rith type, who tried to make their religion into a pagan secret society, he "took the calf which they had made, and burnt it in the fire, and ground it into powder . . . and Moses returned unto the Lord, and said, Oh, this people have sinned a great sin, and made them gods of gold."

The majority of Jews in America during the first generations following independence were opposed to the idea of a Jewish Freemasonic secret society. Thus, Israel Joseph Benjamin, a noted European Jew, in his memoirs *Three Years in America, 1859-62* wrote of the B'nai B'rith that "this is a secret society, like the Freemasons, with passwords and the like and was quite a new phenomenon for me . . . still I think the existence of such a society not at all necessary."

He was right. The secret agenda of the B'nai B'rith—

like that of the Southern Jurisdiction of the Scottish Rite—was to destroy the Union and pave the way for reconquest by Britain.

Benjamin and Belmont

Two leading B'nai B'rith-allied figures would serve as exemplars of the British strategy for permanently dividing the Union: Judah P. Benjamin and August Belmont.

Benjamin (1811-1884) was born in the British West Indies to Sephardic Jewish parents who moved to Charleston, S.C. In 1827, he was inducted into the Charleston Hebrew Orphan Aid Society, one of the precursors of the B'nai B'rith. After attending Yale College in New Haven, Ct. (he was forced to drop out under a cloud of scandal), Benjamin surfaced in New Orleans, where he quickly won the patronage of John Slidell. Slidell, a U.S. senator who would later play a pivotal role in the Confederacy, and sponsored the career of August Belmont, who married Slidell's daughter.

With Slidell's assistance, Benjamin became a prominent attorney, even serving for a period of time as the U.S. attorney for New Orleans. Benjamin gained notoriety for covering up the growing terrorist activities of the Scottish Rite-sponsored Knights of the Golden Circle while serving as the local federal prosecutor. In 1852, Benjamin was elected U.S. senator, a post he retained until the outbreak of the Civil War in 1861, when he resigned to serve the Confederacy. Benjamin was the first Confederate attorney general. He later served as secretary of war and secretary of state, ultimately running the Confederate secret service on behalf of Confederate President Jefferson Davis.

Judah Benjamin escaped to England following the

defeat of the Confederate secessionist plot. It was Benjamin's Confederate secret service which organized and supervised such figures in the assassination of Abraham Lincoln as John Wilkes Booth and his accomplice, John Surratt. Benjamin was charged with sedition for the Lincoln assassination, although he was never brought to trial due to his protected status in England.

With the help of a leading Rothschild political asset in England, Baron Pollack, Benjamin continued his legal career in London. He never abandoned his commitment to subvert and destroy the American republic, however. As a wealthy lawyer for the British merchant oligarchs, Judah Benjamin collaborated with other exiled Confederate and Masonic strategists in England, such as James D. Bulloch and Robert Toombs. Benjamin's continuing preoccupation with defeating Reconstruction is indicated in letters he wrote back to the U.S. with complaints such as these:

"I have always looked with the utmost dread and distrust on the experiment of emancipation so suddenly enforced on the South by the event of the war. God knows how it will all end!"; "the South is kept crushed under negro rule"; "I can never consent to go to New Orleans and break my heart witnessing the rule of negroes and carpetbaggers"; and "nothing is so abhorrent to me as Radicalism which seeks to elevate the populace into the governing class."

The Ku Klux Klan (KKK) was founded in Tennessee in the late 1860s by the southern Scottish Rite leadership under Albert Pike. The KKK drew its membership from the pre-Civil War Knights of the Golden Circle.

Judah P. Benjamin's early role in sponsoring and protecting both the Knights of the Golden Circle and the

Ku Klux Klan offers a crucial insight into the B'nai B'rith-ADL's later role in fostering the revival of the KKK in the post-World War II period. We shall return to that sordid tale in a later chapter.

Another Rothschild and B'nai B'rith ally who enjoyed the political patronage of arch-Confederate John Slidell, August Belmont, was Judah Benjamin's northern counterpart. A private secretary to the British House of Rothschild who arrived in New York City from London in 1837, Belmont rose to the chairmanship of the Democratic Party, a position he held for 20 years. Belmont was a leading advocate of free trade and states' rights, both cornerstones of the British reconquest scheme. Prior to his emergence as a leading figure in the national Democratic Party, Belmont worked closely with the Charleston, S.C. B'nai B'rith in fomenting radicalism among America's youth. The effort was in this case run directly by the Mother Lodge of the Scottish Rite in England, then under the command of Britain's Prime Minister, Lord Palmerston.

At Belmont's behest, Charleston B'nai B'rith leader Edwin DeLeon wrote a pamphlet in the early 1850s entitled *The Position and Duties of Young America*. DeLeon, whose family were slave traders, B'nai B'rith founders and later leading Confederates, peddled free trade and openly advocated a strong Anglo-American alliance. While by today's standards, the appeal for a strong Anglo-American alliance may seem palatable to some, back in the middle of the 19th century, this was borderline treason.

Belmont's Young America members were among the draft rioters and radical abolitionists who disrupted Lincoln's Union war mobilization to the benefit of the

Confederacy and England. During the early phase of the Civil War, England tried repeatedly to intervene into the conflict with "cease fire" plans that would have ensured the permanent dissolution of the Union.

During the Civil War itself, while the majority of American Jews sided with the North and fought valiantly to preserve the Union, the B'nai B'rith was predominantly pro-Confederate. Even in New York City, the Lodges preached secession.

The Baltimore Hebrew Congregation, founded by Dutch Jews who made their money in the slave trade, heard sermons by Rabbi Morris Raphall like the following:

> "Who can blame our brethren of the South for their being inclined to secede from a society under whose government their ends cannot be attained and whose union is kept together by heavy iron ties of violence and arbitrary force? Who can blame our brethren of the South for seceding from a society whose government cannot and will not protect property rights and privileges of a great portion of the Union?"

Following the Civil War and the assassination of President Lincoln, many of the Jewish slave and cotton traders from the South, typified by the Lehman Brothers, moved to New York City and became prominent in Wall Street banking and stock brokerages. With the defeat of President Lincoln's Reconstruction program following his assassination, President Andrew Johnson pardoned the Scottish Rite insurrectionists—including Gen. Albert Pike—and accepted a rank of 32nd Degree in the Southern Jurisdiction Freemasons. Suspected Lincoln assassi-

nation plotter Simon Wolf was also absolved of any criminal culpability for his wartime activities.

The legacy of British Freemasonic treachery against
the Union survived intact—including the B'nai B'rith.

Although the slave trade nominally was banned in
the United States as a result of Lincoln's Emancipation
Proclamation, a new form of slavery had already been
launched by the British East India Company and its Scottish Rite directors, including the same Lord Palmerston
who had played so pivotal a role in the secessionist
insurrection.

The new form of slavery was opium. Henry Carey,
one of the architects of Abraham Lincoln's Reconstruction program and a leading proponent of the American
System of Political Economy, warned about Britain's
Opium War against China and India in his 1853 book
The Slave Trade, Domestic and Foreign. He described
the trade in "that pernicious drug, opium" as "one of
perfect free trade!"

Defeated in the secessionist insurrectionist plot,
Britain and its fifth column of agents in both the North
and the South would eventually regroup around a strategy for running an opium war against the United States.
As the reader will learn in later chapters of this book,
the B'nai B'rith and its Anti-Defamation League "secret
lodge" would play a central role in that effort.

Peddling Slavery Still Today

Fast forward to 1992. In the nation's capital, where B'nai
B'rith lawyer Simon Wolf conspired on behalf of the
southern slave trade, the streets in many parts of town
are dominated now by drug traffickers whose deadly
poison has inflicted both a subculture of addiction and

violence and a spread of the AIDS virus among the predominantly black population. Community-based efforts,
led by the Nation of Islam, have begun to roll back that
new subculture of slavery and despair, restoring safety
and dignity to some of the most desperately poor neighborhoods in the United States.

True to its history, the B'nai B'rith-ADL intercedes
to turn back the clock to the days of slavery.

First, the ADL set off a massive wave of anger and
resentment in the African-American community when,
in June 1992, it published *The Anti-Semitism of Black
Demagogues and Extremists.* The widely circulated ADL
report is a frontal attack on the Nation of Islam (NOI) and
its leader, Minister Louis Farrakhan. It openly threatens
retribution against any elected officials or political activists who "associate with or publicly commend the NOI."

In July 1992, a major uproar developed in Washington, D.C. when the ADL was caught red-handed in an
ugly attempt to shut down any government contact with
what has been the only effective effort to clean up drug-
and crime-infested areas in the nation's capital: the NOI's
now-famous "Dopebusters."

When Washington, D.C. Mayor Sharon Pratt Kelly
issued an official proclamation honoring Nation of Islam
leader Dr. Abdul Alim Muhammad for his leadership in
the Dopebusters campaign, and for his groundbreaking
work in treating AIDS patients with Immuviron, an Afri-
can-developed anti-AIDS drug, the ADL went crazy.

Kelly was repeatedly hit with ADL-organized "delegations" demanding that the proclamation be rescinded
lest she, too, be identified as an anti-Semite. When she
refused, the ADL engaged in a national barrage of media
attacks against the Nation of Islam. The attacks culmi-

nated in an article run in the *Washington Times* coauthored by ADL National Director Abe Foxman and Fact Finding Director Mira Lansky Boland.

Ultimately, Kelly succumbed to ADL demands and issued an "Open Letter to the Community" in which she continued to praise Dr. Muhammad's work against drugs, violence, and AIDS, but condemned alleged "anti-Semitic" statements attributed to him by the ADL.

But what was really at the heart of the *Washington Times* article, which was otherwise a potpourri of outrageous and unsubstantiated charges against the Nation of Islam, was a demand that Congress defeat the major appropriations bill for the Dept. of Housing and Urban Development (HUD), over the question of whether HUD rules should permit a HUD contractor to hire the Dopebusters to provide security for a federally subsidized housing project in Los Angeles. The ADL was particularly upset about the national attention the successful Dopebusters drug eradication program was getting.

The Dopebusters were founded in Washington, D.C. in 1988. Since then, unarmed Dopebuster patrols have been able to eradicate drug trafficking at the street level in nine Washington ghetto neighborhoods and private housing projects. They have done so with no deaths and very little violence.

Exemplary of the success of the program is the Mayfair Mansions housing complex in Northeast Washington. Mayfair Mansions went from an ugly, unsafe, open-air drug market in 1988, to being a handsomely restored, safe, vibrant community, as a result of Dopebuster patrols. When HUD Secretary Jack Kemp visited Mayfair Mansions earlier this year, he admitted that the Nation of Islam's Dopebusters deserved the credit, and indicated that he was open to granting the patrols federal government contracts.

Tenants in public and private housing projects from New York to Baltimore to Los Angeles are demanding Dopebuster patrols. In most cases, the idea has the support of local police and government agencies who have failed to find any other effective way to curtail the intensifying pattern of drug trafficking and violence. In almost every case, the ADL has attempted to block the tenants' choice of security force. Tenant leaders who refuse to back down have been subjected to threats, harassment, break-ins and other forms of intimidation

This time, however, the ADL may have committed a fatal error in launching such an open and vicious attack on the Nation of Islam. Dr. Abdul Alim Muhammad is not only a leader of the NOI, he is one of the most respected community leaders in the Washington area, and his pioneering work against AIDS is gaining him international recognition. The black and Hispanic communities in the U.S. are disproportionately infected by the deadly virus, but have had almost no access to the accepted treatment, which consists of the prohibitively expensive (and highly toxic) AZT, DDI, or DDC.

Dr. Muhammad and New York City physician Dr. Barbara Justice, have reported dramatic success in treating more than 600 patients who are HIV-positive with Immuviron, the drug they brought back from Kenya. The pair is also credited with bringing vital information concerning this new treatment modality to both the general public and the medical profession, taking the point in a courageous effort to avert what would otherwise be the worst holocaust to hit the human race.

Similarly, the ADL's charges against the Dopebusters

carry little credibility, and leave the ADL completely exposed as nothing more than a protection racket for the drug cartel. The Dopebusters enjoy the intense support of the communities they serve and have an unprecedented record of success. Wherever they go, the Dopebusters convey an unmistakable message of hope and inspiration to the community, that the war on drugs *can* be won. Interviews with the residents of the communities served by the Dopebusters make clear that they believe that it is that message, and nothing else, that has made the Nation of Islam and the Dopebusters a target of ADL attack.

In a community where the twin plagues of drug addiction and AIDS are the most visible vestiges of slavery, the ADL has shown that despite the passage of time, its true loyalties lie with the slave masters.

Meyer Lansky, godfather of organized crime.

2 A Public Relations Front for Meyer Lansky

In 1985, the ADL proudly gave its Torch of Liberty award to Las Vegas "businessman" Morris Barney Dalitz. The award ceremony, a strictly black-tie affair, was given front-page attention in the League's monthly *Bulletin*, which praised Dalitz as a great philanthropist who had donated generously to the ADL over the years.

Dalitz's "generosity" was motivated by a lot more than an impulse to help out a favorite charity. As one of the most important figures in organized crime over a period of sixty years, and as a lifetime right-hand man to organized crime's 20th-century "chairman of the board," Meyer Lansky, Moe Dalitz was well aware of the fact that the Anti-Defamation League was, from its founding, a powerful secret arm of the National Crime Syndicate. Without the ADL's undaunted "public relations" work on behalf of organized crime, the United States would have never been flooded with illegal drugs, and gangsters like Dalitz and Lansky would have long ago been carted off to the penitentiary. Dalitz was one of the kingpins of the Prohibition-era bootlegging business. He, along with three other gangsters, Morris Kleinman, Sam Tucker, and Louis Rothkopf, ran the Cleveland underworld. Their self-described "Jewish Navy" smuggled rotgut whiskey across the Great Lakes from Canada into the Midwest United States.

On the Canadian side of the lakes, the booze was manufactured by the Bronfman Gang, led by Sam and Abe Bronfman, second-generation Romanian immigrants whose father had been brought over to Canada by the B'nai B'rith-allied Baron de Hirsch Fund and had set up a string of whorehouses. Sam and Abe used their Pure Drug Company, which was established with the help of the Hudson's Bay Company, to manufacture illegal whiskey during the Canadian Prohibition (1915-19). When Canada legalized booze and the U.S. instituted its ban a year later, they were all ready to become the major suppliers to the gangsters south of the border.

U.S. government documents from the Prohibition era claim that over 34,000 Americans died of alcohol poisoning drinking the Bronfman brew. Today, Sam Bronfman's son Edgar is a national commissioner of the ADL and the head of its powerful New York Appeal. We will pick up the trail of Edgar Bronfman later in our story.

Following Prohibition, Moe Dalitz became the undisputed crime boss of Cleveland, expanding his criminal operations (gambling, labor racketeering, money laundering, tax evasion) from Hollywood and Las Vegas to

Miami. One of his Miami "investments," a nightspot called the Frolic Club, was a joint venture with Lansky.

When Lansky moved into Cuba to open his first offshore gambling, narcotics, and money laundering haven, Dalitz was brought in as a privileged partner. When Lansky and the other directors of the National Crime Syndicate decided that his longtime partner Benjamin "Bugsy" Siegel had become a liability and had to be assassinated, it was Dalitz who assumed the lion's share of Siegel's Las Vegas casino interests—interests he still holds today.

Lansky and Siegel had formed the original Murder, Inc.—otherwise known as the "Meyer and Bugsy Gang"—to enforce the creation of a National Crime Syndicate overseeing the Prohibition-era illegal liquor and narcotics traffic. From the very outset, Dalitz had been a member of the national commission of the crime syndicate. Up until Lansky's death in 1983, Dalitz was a regular visitor to the crime boss's Miami Beach condo, and was widely presumed by law enforcement officials to be one of the primary heirs to Lansky's crime empire.

Just two years after Lansky's death, Dalitz was publicly surfaced as an ADL philanthropist. It was a sign of the times. By the beginning of the 1980's "Decade of Greed," drug money—narco-dollars—had already replaced petro-dollars as the primary source of liquidity to fuel the stock market and real estate speculative bubbles facilitated by the Carter and Reagan administrations' deregulation of the banking and brokerage industries. As the power of drug money grew, so too did the political and financial clout of the ADL. Junk bond swindlers like Ivan Boesky and Michael Milken, and dope bankers like

Edmund Safra—not to mention Moe Dalitz—regularly poured millions into the ADL war chest. In return for this largesse, the ADL publicly branded anyone who challenged the clout of organized crime as a dyed in the wool anti-Semite.

The lionizing of mobster Dalitz was the ADL's way of boasting that their public relations work over a seventy-year period had paid off.

Gangsters and Traitors from the Start

Things were not always so easy.

The ADL had been founded shortly after the turn of the century as a "Jewish defense" arm of the B'nai B'rith, the nominally Jewish secret society sponsored and controlled by the Scottish Rite of Freemasonry and by some of the leading British and American WASP families.

B'nai B'rith Washington, D.C. representative Simon Wolf, the man whom Lincoln's Secret Service Chief LaFayette C. Baker had arrested as a Confederate spy and Union blockade runner during the Civil War, was now working closely with President Theodore Roosevelt in mobilizing Jewish-American support for the overthrow of the Russian Czar.

According to Wolf's 1918 autobiography, he had met secretly with President Roosevelt at his Sagamore Hills estate in New York and had launched an international drive to brand the Czarist regime as "anti-Semitic." After a series of meetings and correspondence with Russia's Prime Minister Count Sergei Witte (arranged by Roosevelt), Wolf had denounced the Russian regime for reneging on its promises to curb anti-Jewish pogroms, after which American Jewish organizations, led from behind the scenes by the B'nai B'rith, began funneling guns to the anti-Czarist insurrectionists. Thus, B'nai B'rith played an active role in the Russian Revolution of 1905.

This activity would lead to widespread allegations that prominent American Jews were pro-Bolshevik. The Warburg family of Kuhn, Loeb and Company did fund V.I. Lenin and Leon Trotsky; and father and son Bolshevik agents Julius and Armand Hammer, who helped found the U.S. Communist Party, did actively spread the Bolshevik cause in America and spent a decade in the Soviet Union following the 1917 Revolution. These allegations of pro-Communist sentiments, while grounded in well-publicized, scandalous actions by prominent Jewish families, missed the mark.

In fact, the plot to bring down the Czar and install the Bolsheviks in power in Russia served longstanding British imperial and geopolitical interests of the sort advanced by the Scottish Rite. Britain feared the development of a Eurasian alliance among France, Germany, Russia, Japan, and China, based on economic cooperation and facilitated by the building of a transcontinental system of railroads linking the East to the West. Such a transcontinental railroad system would render Britain's domination over the seas relatively unimportant.

B'nai B'rith joined in the effort to sink the Czar for the same reasons the Order joined in the Confederates' secessionist plot to destroy the Union forty years earlier: because B'nai B'rith was an arm of the British Freemasonic treason.

In fact, one of the most compelling reasons for British hatred of Russia was the role played by Czar Alexander II in coming to the aid of Abraham Lincoln during the darkest days of the U.S. Civil War. In 1863, Czar Alexander dispatched the powerful Russian Navy to the

U.S. ports of New York and San Francisco and threatened to go to war against Britain if the Crown joined the war on the side of the Confederacy.

At the same time the so-called Jewish-Bolshevik ties were being targeted (frequently by people with actual anti-Semitic biases), diligent local police around the United States were becoming legitimately alarmed at the growing crime problem. New York City Police Commissioner Theodore A. Bingham, in September 1908, penned an article for the prestigious *North American Review* titled "Foreign Criminals in New York." The article detailed the rise of gambling, prostitution and drugs on New York's Lower East Side, emphasizing the role of Jewish, Italian and Irish immigrant gangsters in that crime explosion.

Bingham was not alone in his concern about the rise of gangsterism in the Jewish communities of the metropolitan New York area and beyond. In April 1910, the leading Jewish families of the United States, Germany, France and Great Britain sent delegates to a "Jewish International Convention on the Suppression of the Traffic in Girls and Women" in London. Keynote speaker Arthur R. Moro delivered an alarming report on the involvement of Jewish gangsters in the worldwide white slave trade and in bigtime prostitution:

"I wish I had time to tell you all I know, which goes to show that the traffic of Jewesses is almost worldwide. But I must restrict myself to a few . . . incidents to prove that an extensive traffic does exist. . . . In 1901, a Rabbi came from the Transvaal and told me that the amount of Jewish prostitution and traffic in Johannesburg, Pretoria, Lourenco Marques, Beira and Salisbury are appalling. In later years, the same story came from another Rabbi regarding Capetown. . . . In 1903, a Jewish schoolmaster who had spent some time in Egypt said that the traffic by Jews of Jewesses to Alexandria, Cairo and Port Said was an absolute scandal. There were Greek, Italian and French prostitutes, but they were far outnumbered by the Jewesses. . . . We have received, and have correspondence to show that this awful condition of affairs exists in Calcutta to a large extent, and also all along the free ports of China. . . . From the Chief Rabbi of Constantinople, from a distinguished Jewish-American scholar, from a prominent London gentleman, and from a schoolmistress in Calata we have had letters during the past six months describing an outrageous condition of affairs in Constantinople, where traffic in prostitutes is carried out openly and shamelessly, and where the traffickers have their own Synagogue. . . . They say things in Damascus are even worse."

Already in 1909, the leading "Our Crowd" families of New York had established their own Bureau of Social Morals, headed by Rabbi Judah P. Magnes. The Bureau hired private detective Abe Schoenfeld, an investigator for John D. Rockefeller, Jr., to infiltrate and profile the organized crime structure centered on the Lower East Side of Manhattan. Schoenfeld's mission was hardly that of crimebuster. In 1922, Rabbi Magnes took those voluminous files with him when he moved to Jerusalem and founded the Hebrew University. To this day, that genealogical chart of organized crime remains a part of the university's most closely guarded archives. It was during this same period of mounting concern over the exposure of Jewish-surnamed gangsters, that the Anti-Defamation League was founded.

One of the very first targets of the ADL was New York Police Commissioner Bingham, whom the ADL smeared as an anti-Semite for his efforts to quell organized crime on the Lower East Side. Bingham's crime-fighting efforts were by no means targeted exclusively against Jewish gangsters. His chief detective, Lt. Joseph Petrosino, was assassinated in March 1909 in Sicily, while meeting with Italian police to establish cooperation in probing links between criminal elements and anarchist networks operating in both the United States and Italy.

In 1901, Petrosino had warned the Secret Service about an imminent assassination attempt against President William McKinley. Petrosino had learned of the plot by infiltrating his agents into the Henry Street Settlement House in New York, a hotbed of British Fabian Society and international anarchist activity. The Secret Service ignored his warnings, and McKinley was assassinated months later, leaving British agent and B'nai B'rith ally Teddy Roosevelt to assume the presidency.

The nascent ADL, still formally called the Publicity Committee of the B'nai B'rith, had assailed Bingham's crimefighting efforts for "maligning Jews" and eventually succeeded in having him ousted as police commissioner. Organized crime got a big boost as a result. What's more, the effort to establish the links between organized crime, international anarchist circles and, perhaps, the Scottish Rite and B'nai B'rith secret societies, was stillborn.

The man who founded and headed up the ADL for its first thirty years was Sigmund Livingston, a prominent Chicago attorney who had headed up the powerful B'nai B'rith Midwest Lodge Number 6. Livingston was the lawyer for the Chicago and Alton Railways, a company owned by William Moore of the prominent Episcopalian family. From the 1890s, the Moore family had forged a business alliance with the J.P. Morgan banking interests.

The Moores, with Morgan financing, founded the National Biscuit Company (now RJR-Nabisco) and U.S. Steel Corporation. Within two generations, members of the Moore family would also control Bankers Trust Company and sit on the board of the International Business Machines Corporation (IBM).

The Moore family's sponsorship of Livingston, ADL chairman from 1913-45, was a reflection of the underlying relationship between the leading WASP Freemasonic families and the ADL that continues through to the present. The Moore family's Nabisco and U.S. Steel are on record today as major financial backers of the ADL.

Ironically, Bishop Paul Moore, of the same Moore family, served for years as the Episcopal Bishop of New York, based at the Cathedral of St. John the Divine. He was the superior to Canon Edward West.

Canon West's promise to "get his Jewish friends to take care of" Lyndon LaRouche provided crucial evidence that the real power behind the ADL and its organized crime confederates is the Scottish Rite.

Prohibition

With the ADL's successful drive to oust New York Police Commissioner Bingham, organized crime began to spread its tentacles out into New York City and across the country. By the onset of Prohibition in 1920, the undisputed chief of the New York rackets was Arnold Rothstein, the son of a prominent garment manufacturer and a junior member of the elite "Our Crowd."

Many of the "Our Crowd" families—like the Lehmans—had come to New York from the South in the post-Civil War period. They were transplanted Confederates who capitalized on the power of the British Roth-

schild family's Wall Street representative, August Belmont, to quickly establish themselves among the city's
leading bankers and stockbrokers. They had participated
in the unsuccessful Confederate secessionist plot against
the Union. Now, they would take a leading role in the
British effort to direct a new opium war against the
American people.

Rothstein operated a gambling and prostitution syn-
dicate out of the Metropole Hotel in Midtown Manhattan,
far from the teeming ethnic ghetto of the Lower East Side.
He ran the unofficial gambling commission for Tammany
Hall boss Timothy Sullivan. He hobnobbed with some
of the country's wealthiest legitimate businessmen, like
Julius Fleischmann, the yeast manufacturer, Joseph Seagram, the Canadian distiller, Harry Sinclair of the Sinclair
Oil Company, and Percival H. Hill, head of the American
Tobacco Company. In 1919, Rothstein engineered the
fixing of the baseball World Series on behalf of his gam-
bling cronies, in what became known as the Chicago
"Black Sox" scandal.

At the behest of Lower East Side gangster Irving
Wexler (also known as Waxey Gordon) and Detroit
mobster Max Greenberg, Rothstein put up the initial
$175,000 to establish the first bootlegging operations of
the Prohibition era, servicing the Midwest and the East
Coast with British whiskey transported across the Atlan-
tic. Rum running ships owned by Rothstein and his part-
ners would smuggle the British whiskey from Long Island
Sound into the U.S. Rothstein's British contacts included
Winston Churchill, who at the time headed the Royal
Commission in charge of liquor.

In 1921, Rothstein also opened up a British pipeline
for smuggling heroin into the United States, via his busi-

ness agent in China, Jacob Katzenberg. Katzenberg hooked up with the British opium cartel, then headed by Lord Keswick of the Hongkong and Shanghai Banking Corporation and the Jardine and Matheson trading company, and arranged the transit of the illegal drugs through Marseilles into New York City. The route, later known as the "French Connection," would remain the primary pipeline of heroin into America up through the 1960s.

ADL Gets a Piece of the Action

The period of Prohibition marked the syndication of organized crime. It also marked the emergence of illegal money as a major source of investment capital in so-called legitimate business. As the proceeds of the billions of dollars in illegal whiskey and dope sales were funneled into such lucrative "straight" investments as the Hollywood motion picture and music industries, the Nevada gambling casinos (Nevada conveniently legalized casino gambling just as Prohibition was coming to an end), and post-Prohibition legal alcohol distilleries, the ADL was on hand to directly reap the benefits.

In 1929, one of Meyer Lansky's New York City crime lieutenants, Frank Erickson, founded the Sterling National Bank. Erickson was a specialist in money laundering. After Lansky replaced Arnold Rothstein (he was assassinated in 1926) as the chairman of the board of the National Crime Syndicate, Erickson had been put in charge of the nationwide bookmaking operations. Erickson handled Lansky's hidden interests in gambling casinos, racetracks and other businesses around the country. Sterling National Bank served as the mob's "factor" bank in the New York City garment center, doling out high-interest, short-term loans to thousands of small clothing manufacturers to purchase their raw materials.

The loans were collateralized by the garment firms' accounts receivable. On paper, it was a "benign," barely legal form of loan sharking. In practice, it was the syndicate's foot in the door for taking over the entire garment industry through violence and intimidation. Erickson's relationship with Lansky gave Sterling virtually unchallenged control over the garment center. In 1934, Theodore H. Silbert went to work for Sterling National Bank. Within a decade of his arrival, Silbert was the bank's chairman, president, and CEO, posts he would retain up until his death in early 1992.

Silbert was the ADL's man on the scene. He would serve as the ADL's national commissioner, treasurer, and chief fundraiser. The ADL established its bank accounts at Sterling National, and, according to IRS records, invested in bank stock. The only other outside investment into which the ADL would ever put its own money would be the American Bank and Trust Company (ABT), another New York City bank which listed ADL National Commissioner and B'nai B'rith International President Philip Klutznick as a director. ABT would go under when shady Mossad financier David Graiver made off with all the bank's deposits and then ostensibly died in a mysterious airplane crash over Mexico. Graiver's so-called death was so suspect that New York State listed him as a co-conspirator in the ABT bank fraud investigation for years.

Although Silbert's emergence as the leading figure at Sterling National was part of a campaign to cleanse the bank's public image by replacing a known gangster with a "philanthropist and civic-minded banker," Sterling continued to be entangled in shady financial dealings, sometimes leading to high-visibility civil suits. The most explosive of these scandals hit in January 1982, when the Italian government filed suit in U.S. District Court in New York City against Sterling, charging it with "constructive trust, conspiracy to defraud, fraud, and breach of fiduciary duty." The case revolved around Italian banker Michele Sindona's looting of $27 million from the Banca Privata in 1973-74. The theft had repercussions across the Atlantic as well. The Franklin National Bank on Long Island, N.Y. went bust as the result of Sindona's involvement. Sterling National Bank was one of the laundromats through which Sindona washed the stolen cash.

Not surprisingly, Sindona would later be exposed as a pivotal figure in the Propaganda-2 Freemasonic Lodge, a secret Italian branch of the Scottish Rite with strong ties to the Mafia. Its antecedent, the 19th-century Propaganda-1 Lodge, had been founded by Giuseppe Mazzini, the founder of the Sicilian Mafia, a leading member of the First Communist International and an agent of Britain's Lord Palmerston, the Grand Master of the Scottish Rite.

Some things just never change.

ADL's shady links to Sterling National Bank went beyond Theodore Silbert. Another longtime director of the bank and ADL man, Maxwell Raab, was a business partner of Meyer Lansky in a company called the International Airport Hotel Corporation. The vice chairman of the powerful New York State ADL, Raab weathered the public airing of his Lansky links and went on to be the United States ambassador to Italy during the Reagan administration.

Arnold Burns was another ADL asset on the board of Sterling. Burns's law firm, Burns and Summit, got caught up in a tax evasion scheme in the early 1980s that almost landed both partners in jail. Under a loophole in the federal tax codes written into law thanks to the Zionist lobby in the U.S. Congress, American investors in Israeli research and development firms could claim their investments as tax writeoffs.

Arnold Burns set up a string of tax shelters in the Bahamas, ostensibly to fund these Israeli R&D projects. However, the money—minus a hefty fee to Burns and Summit—never reached Israel. It was laundered right back into the U.S. where it could be used by its owners, tax free. When the scheme became the subject of a federal grand jury in New York, Burns pointed a finger at some of his cohorts and walked away unscathed. A few months later, Arnold Burns was named deputy attorney general of the United States, a post he held throughout most of the Reagan era! Burns's name had been placed before Ronald Reagan by John J. McCloy, a powerhouse in the New York City WASP establishment, and the former chairman of Chase Manhattan Bank.

Nor is Sterling National Bank the only ADL bank implicated in the dope trade and organized crime. Leonard Abess of Miami, Fla., is another honorary national chairman of the ADL. He is the chairman of City National Bank of Miami, one of many Florida banks caught laundering bigtime drug money. A top aide to Abess at City National, Alberto Duque, was jailed in the late 1980s for laundering dope dollars. Another senior bank official, Donald Beasley, was hired by Abess on the basis of his former work for the Nugen Hand Bank in Australia.

Nugen Hand went bust in the mid-1980s when one of its founders, Frank Nugen, was found dead in his car, the victim of what police labeled a "suicide," and the other partner, former Green Beret and CIA agent Michael Hand, disappeared into thin air with $26 million in bank assets. Nugen Hand had been set up during the final days of the Vietnam War by ex-CIA and Pentagon officers, including Ted Shackley, to launder black market profits into shady intelligence operations throughout Asia.

Hollywood Hoodlums

If the 1985 Moe Dalitz award dinner was a kind of "coming out party" for the ADL's friends in the National Crime Syndicate, it was by no means the first time the League publicly flaunted its deep ties to the gangster world.

In 1963, as part of an effort to vastly expand its fundraising reach, the ADL appointed Hollywood producer Dore Schary as its national chairman. At the time, Schary was the reigning superstar at the Metro Goldwyn Mayer studios. Among the Hollywood insiders, however, Schary was known as a lifelong pal of syndicate higher-up Abner "Longie" Zwillman of New Jersey. Zwillman was one of the first of the Prohibition-era bootleggers and Lansky aides to get involved in the Hollywood motion picture industry. An original member of "Murder, Inc." and the head of the powerful Reinfeld bootlegging syndicate in New Jersey, Zwillman expanded into labor racketeering during the waning days of Prohibition. By 1930, he had seized control over the screen operators union up and down the East Coast, and parlayed that into shares in some of the big Hollywood studios.

At this time, Dore Schary ran an amateur drama group at the YMHA in Newark, N.J. Childhood friend Zwillman sent Schary out to the West Coast and installed him at MGM.

When Zwillman got into trouble with the IRS in

the late 1950s, some of his syndicate associates became convinced that he might betray some of the mob's most closely held financial secrets. On Feb. 27, 1959, he was found hanging from a pipe in the basement of his twenty-room West Orange, N.J. mansion. According to FBI reports, Schary attended the funeral. In the FBI memo citing Schary's appearance at the Zwillman funeral, the Bureau delivered a kind of eulogy to the mobster. Citing an article from the *New York World Telegram,* the FBI memo read:

"Nobody . . . followed so successfully for so long the approved underworld formula for success—from rags to rackets to riches to respectability."

If the "rags to respectability" formula were to be applied to organizations, the Anti-Defamation League would be first on the list of success stories.

EIRNS/Leo Scanlon

ADL executive Kenneth Bialkin, attorney for organized crime drug money laundering figures.

3 The ADL and the Opium War Against America

For the past two decades, Wall Street lawyer Kenneth Bialkin has been "Mr. ADL." A longstanding member of the League's National Executive Committee, Bialkin served from 1982 through 1986 as the League's national chairman. It was on his watch that gangster Moe Dalitz got the ADL's prestigious "Torch of Liberty" prize; that junk bond swindler Michael Milken poured millions of dollars into the launching of the League's "A World of Difference" propaganda campaign to wreck American public education; and that accused drug money launderer Edmund Safra got Bialkin and the ADL to mediate a corporate divorce between his banking empire and the American Express Company. In return for Bialkin's effort to salvage Safra's badly tarnished reputation, the ADL received a $1 million tax-exempt payoff from him.

But Bialkin's real claim to fame is that he was a central figure in the doping of America. Without Kenneth Bialkin's behind the scenes legal maneuvering, the Medellín Cartel would have had a far more difficult time establishing a beachhead in the United States. In much the same way Bialkin quieted the potentially stormy divorce between Edmund Safra and American Express, he brokered the marriage between renegade financier Robert Vesco and the Medellín Cartel's chief of logistics, Carlos Lehder Rivas. As a result, the dope smuggling routes through the Caribbean into the United States were consolidated, and the streets of America were flooded during the 1980s with marijuana and cocaine.

Bialkin, Vesco, and IOS

This sordid story began in 1970, when Kenneth Bialkin, the senior partner at the Wall Street law firm of Willkie, Farr and Gallagher, helped engineer Robert Vesco's take-over of the Investors Overseas Service (IOS), a Swiss-based mutual fund that was founded by Bernie Cornfeld with startup funding from the Swiss-French branch of the Rothschild family.

IOS was a front for Meyer Lansky's international crime syndicate. IOS "salesmen" traveled the globe carrying suitcases full of cash across international borders. Some of the money came from local investors, but the bulk of it was hot money gained from the Lansky syndicate's dope, gambling, prostitution, and extortion rackets.

If this method of money laundering was labor intensive and primitive compared to today's high-speed electronic wire transfers, it was nevertheless efficient. The cash eventually wound up in numbered accounts at some of Switzerland's most corrupt and secretive banks. Some of the banks linked to the IOS apparatus, like the Geneva-based International Credit Bank (BCI) and the Nassau, Bahamas-based Bank of World Commerce, were flagrant fronts for the Lansky syndicate. While BCI was owned by a senior officer of the Israeli Mossad named Tibor Rosenbaum, BCI's office manager, Sylvain Ferdman, was identified by *Life* magazine in 1967 as one of Lansky's top bagmen; and World Commerce director Alvin Malnik was Lansky's "accountant."

When Lansky and his controllers decided to shift the center of their underground banking operations from Switzerland to the Caribbean as part of the planned expansion of cocaine and marijuana smuggling into the United States, it was the ADL and Bialkin that engineered the move.

First, the ADL's Minneapolis, Minn. apparatus (known inside the League as the "Minneapolis Mafia"), which ran the notorious Kid Cann (Isadore Blumenfeld) organized crime ring, provided the money for a local Hebrew schoolteacher turned business entrepreneur named Meshulam Riklis to buy up a large block of shares of IOS stock. Once Riklis had amassed enough stock to control the company, he turned around and sold all his shares to Vesco. Vesco was represented in the transaction by Kenneth Bialkin.

Vesco's next step was to oust Bernie Cornfeld as the president of IOS and take over the job himself. Over the next several years, a total of $270 million was siphoned out of IOS accounts in Switzerland. Officially, the money was never found, and Robert Vesco conveniently fled the United States one step ahead of the FBI and the IRS.

The Cornfeld to Riklis to Vesco transaction itself

may have been largely a wash of Lansky syndicate dollars. From Prohibition onward, the Minneapolis Kid Cann gang had been handlers of Lansky money. Kid Cann eventually moved to the Miami area and was a key player in Lansky's bigtime move into southern Florida "gold coast" real estate.

However, not all of the money siphoned out of IOS by Vesco was "family cash." A lawsuit was brought in U.S. District Court in New York City in 1980 by some of the independent investors who had lost their shirts in the looting of IOS. While not revealing the whereabouts of the missing millions, the civil suit identified Bialkin and the Bank of New York as partners of the fugitive financier in the scheme. On July 31, 1980, Federal Judge D.J. Stewart ordered Willkie, Farr and Gallagher to pay $24.5 million to a group of IOS investors and ordered the Bank of New York to pay $35.6 million. The case file, which fills twenty cartons stored at the Federal District Court warehouse in Bayonne, N.J., shows that Bialkin was the evil genius behind the looting scheme.

A year before the court ordered Willkie, Farr and the Bank of New York to pay up for their role in the looting of IOS, some of that money had been used by Vesco to purchase Normans Cay in the Bahamas. Vesco's partner in the deal was Carlos Lehder Rivas, a small-time Colombian car thief and marijuana smuggler who had recently gotten out of jail in Florida. Lehder, an unabashed supporter of Adolf Hitler who would later use some of his smuggling profits to found a neo-Nazi, radical environmentalist political party in Colombia, fit neatly into the ADL scheme, with his family ties back in Colombia to leading figures in the then-emerging Medellín Cartel.

By 1980, the Vesco-Lehder-owned Normans Cay was serving as the command center and transshipment depot for a massive marijuana and cocaine trafficking operation from Medellín into the United States.

For several years, while running the Normans Cay operation, Vesco skipped from the Bahamas to Costa Rica to Nicaragua, buying up local politicians and newspaper editors and always miraculously staying one step ahead of an FBI that never really seemed too intent on capturing the fugitive money man. On one occasion on Antigua, Vesco was hosting a lavish party on a boat that he had bought from Saudi financier Adnan Khashoggi, while FBI agents were combing the island looking for the elusive fugitive.

In 1982, Vesco took more secure permanent refuge in Havana, Cuba as the personal guest and financial adviser to Communist dictator Fidel Castro. Vesco and Lehder cut Castro into the lucrative cocaine and marijuana business, using Cuban airstrips to refuel their drug flights to America and, in return, helping Fidel to funnel guns to terrorist groups across Latin America. According to investigative reporter Ernest Volkman, by 1984, Vesco and Lehder had earned Fidel a $20 billion cut of the growing Western Hemisphere dope trade. Thanks to ADL frontman Vesco, Americans were getting hooked on cocaine, while Fidel Castro was reaping billions to foment narco-terrorist insurgencies all over the Hemisphere.

In the meantime, back on U.S. soil, "Mr. ADL," Kenneth Bialkin, continued to ply his trade. In 1988, he left his post as managing partner of Willkie, Farr to take a partnership at another Wall Street mega-firm, Skadden Arps Slate Meagher and Flom. In the speculative frenzy that had followed the Carter administration's deregulation of the nation's banking system and financial markets, Skadden Arps had emerged as the "sleaze king" of Wall Street lawyering. The firm's number one client was Drexel Burnham's junk bond super-salesman, Michael Milken. When Milken left the wood-paneled conference rooms of lower Manhattan to set up shop in Beverly Hills, Calif., Skadden Arps obliged by opening up their own eighty-man Beverly Hills office to service Milken's every need.

Among Milken's oldest and most well-fed clients was Meshulam Riklis, the former Minneapolis Hebrew schoolteacher who had been an important prop in the Bialkin-executed takeover and looting of IOS.

(To do him justice, it should be noted that before he landed in Minnesota, the Turkish-born Riklis had been a British police spy in Palestine before Israel won its independence. When his treachery was exposed, the Stern Gang, led by Menachem Begin and Yitzhak Shamir, had imposed a death sentence on Riklis. That death sentence was finally lifted in the early 1980s after the Begin and Shamir-led Likud Party came into power in Israel, and Riklis made a very large cash contribution to their campaign coffers. That rapprochement was apparently arranged by Israel's Defense Minister Ariel Sharon, after Riklis bought him a ranch in the Negev Desert.)

Bialkin and Safra

Before he moved over to Skadden Arps, Kenneth Bialkin had occupied a great deal of his time during the 1980s with engineering a consolidation and reorganization of some of the oldest of the "Our Crowd" brokerage houses. The banking deregulation frenzy of the Carter and early Reagan years, combined with skyrocketing U.S. interest rates, had turned the U.S. economy into a haven for hot money. "Narco-dollars" were flooding the U.S., and Bialkin apparently recognized that if he could create a large enough and diversified enough financial structure to accommodate the hot cash, the rewards would be nearly endless.

In rapid succession, he executed the absorption of Lehman Brothers into Kuhn, Loeb and Company. Shearson Hayden Stone bought out Loeb Rhodes. And, by 1984, all of those houses had been in turn bought out by American Express Company, which changed its name to Shearson Lehman American Express.

Bialkin was an attorney of record on each of these transactions and he landed a seat on the board of directors of the newly consolidated Shearson Amex entity. Bialkin's buddy Henry Kissinger, by now a high-flying consultant to a fleet of major multinational corporations, also joined the board of the Amex mega-combine.

In 1983, Bialkin had also orchestrated the marriage of the Amex conglomerate with Edmund Safra's Trade Development Bank of Geneva. When the ink dried, Safra was holding 4 percent of Amex's stock and was president of its private banking division. The other large-block shareholder in the new conglomerate was Carl Lindner, another rags-to-riches wheeler-dealer long suspected of being a front man for the Lansky crowd. Courtesy of Michael Milken and former Dalitz "Purple Gang" member Max Fisher (another prominent ADL figure), Lindner became the owner of United Brands, formerly the United Fruit Company. U.S. Drug Enforcement Administration officials acknowledged in 1978 that an estimated 20 percent of the illegal drugs coming into the United States from South and Central America were being smuggled courtesy of United Brands, a company with longstanding ties to organized crime and U.S. intelligence.

The capacity for money laundering and smuggling represented by this United Brands-Amex combine made Vesco's earlier IOS venture seem like a mom and pop operation in comparison.

However, things began to unravel very dramatically for Bialkin and his conglomerate clients on April 2, 1989. That day's Sunday edition of New York *Newsday* ran a full-page banner headline: "Dirty Money—No. 606347712 Is the NY Bank Account Where 2 Major Drug Money-Laundering Probes Meet."

The story, by ace investigative reporter Knut Royce, revealed that Edmund Safra's Republic National Bank of New York was serving as a money laundering hub for both the Medellín Cartel and the Syrian-Lebanese Mafia. DEA and U.S. Customs investigators involved in two separate high-priority probes had traced dope dollars from South America and the Middle East into the same numbered account at the main branch of Republic.

Royce's story was based in part on a Jan. 3, 1989 DEA report from the Berne, Switzerland office. The subject of the report was a Geneva-based firm, Shakarchi Trading Company. Working in league with the Bulgarian secret police, the Turkish mafia, and Syrian and Lebanese drug traffickers in the Bekaa Valley, Shakarchi had laundered the profits of the Middle East heroin and hashish trade through Switzerland into Republic National Bank. Account No. 606347712 was Shakarchi's account.

What's more, the DEA document revealed that Edmund Safra had been a lifelong friend of Mahmoud Shakarchi, the founder of the Swiss company, and continued to enjoy a close business relationship with Mahmoud's sons, who were running the firm at the time of the *Newsday* exposé. The DEA report said that all of Safra's banks had "surfaced in the investigation of Shakarchi's alleged drug money laundering activities."

The *Newsday* story had been apparently put together with the assistance of angry federal drug investigators who felt that major drug money laundering cases had been blocked for political reasons.

Indeed, both Bialkin and Safra were hot political commodities at that moment. Iran-Contra special prosecutor Lawrence Walsh was deep into his probe of illegal covert operations by the Reagan-Bush White House, and both Bialkin and Safra—as well as the ADL—had surfaced as prominent players in the secret diplomacy with Khomeini's Iran and the illegal covert war against Nicaragua:

• Bialkin had been the attorney for Adnan Khashoggi in arranging for the Saudi financier's purchasing of the original shipment of arms to Iran in exchange for the release of an American hostage.

• Bialkin's Willkie, Farr law partner in Geneva, Willard Zucker, had been the money handler for Oliver North and Richard Secord at Lake Resources, Inc. Earlier, Zucker had been Bialkin's Swiss point-man in the Vesco looting of IOS.

• Another longtime Wall Street associate of Bialkin, Arthur Liman, had served as the chief counsel to the Senate Iran-Contra panel, which whitewashed the scandal and threw up major roadblocks to Walsh's independent counsel probe.

• The ADL's Latin American Affairs director, Rabbi Morton Rosenthal, had authored a report labeling the Sandinista regime in Nicaragua as "anti-Semitic" and urging all American Jews to back the Reagan administration's secret war in Central America.

- Carl Gershman, who cut his political teeth working as a full-time staffer at the ADL's Fact Finding (dirty tricks) Division in the late 1960s, was made the head of the Reagan administration's National Endowment for Democracy (NED), which was the primary funding conduit for the entire Contra effort.

- Edmund Safra had been directly involved in the logistics of the Iran-Contra operations through his Republic Corporate Air front company, which he jointly owned with Willard Zucker. According to news accounts, it was one of Safra's airplanes that brought Ollie North and Robert McFarlane to Teheran in the spring of 1986 on their last ill-fated effort at an arms-for-hostage deal.

The *Newsday* story also intersected an escalating war of words between Safra and Amex Chairman James Robinson III. Safra had quit as Amex's international banking head a few years after he had merged his Trade Development Bank into the Bialkin-made mega-firm. With a four-year, non-competition clause now expired, Safra had launched a raid on some of Amex's top employees and private banking clients in preparation for the launching of a new private bank in Switzerland. Amex fought back and the whole sordid affair landed before a federal judge in civil court in New York. Kenneth Bialkin, still representing Amex, hammered out an out of court settlement which included a published apology to Safra and a payment by Amex of $1 million to each of four of Safra's favorite "charities." The ADL was on the top of the list of beneficiaries.

It was a classic case of ADL sleight of hand. Amex delivered an "apology" to Safra, "exonerating" Safra of any alleged drug money laundering, even though nobody ever challenged the authenticity of either the DEA's Berne memo or the *Newsday* story! The *New York Times* and all the major Wall Street-linked news media dutifully ran the Amex *mea culpa,* and the ADL waltzed off with a cool million bucks in tax-exempt funds.

In the meantime, the ADL was busy on a dozen other fronts, helping to fuel the speculative frenzy that would drive the U.S. economy into the ground by the end of the 1980s.

Convicted insider trader Michael Milken, who has close ADL ties, used a network of "corporate raiders" to launder money through his junk bond schemes.

4 The ADL and the Junk Bond Bandits Rip Off America

In the autumn of 1991, attorney Alan Dershowitz, who had been hired by junk bond king Michael Milken to get him out of jail, purchased an ad in the *New York Times* to denounce a new book on Milken as "anti-Semitic." The book, *Den of Thieves* by James B. Stewart, the front-page editor of the *Wall Street Journal,* detailed the massive and consistent criminality of Milken's operation at Drexel Burnham.

In his book, Stewart cut through the myth of Milken as a financial genius, showing instead that much of his "success" was due to illegal acts which preyed upon both those who invested their money with Drexel's brokers, and on the U.S. economy as a whole.

The attempt by Dershowitz to dismiss Milken's criminality by alleging that he was the victim of an "anti-

Semitic cabal" was vintage ADL. In much the same way that the League cut its teeth defending Lower East Side gangsters against the crackdown by New York City Police Commissioner Theodore Bingham by libeling the commissioner as an unrepentant "anti-Semite," Dershowitz and other ADL mouthpieces branded Milken's accusers with the same devastating label.

The Dershowitz defense of Milken let slip a very important secret: Milken and his Wall Street allies had replaced the pinstripe-suited and machinegun-toting gangsters of Prohibition as the lions of organized crime. It was Meyer Lansky's dream come true: to insulate his organized crime successors as "untouchables" by putting them in the driver's seat of the U.S. economy. And the ADL was on hand every step along the way.

Recycling Narco-Dollars

When Milken, fresh out of the Wharton School of Economics at the University of Pennsylvania, first presented his theories on the profitability of high-yield bonds (also known as junk bonds) to skeptical traders at Drexel Burnham in the early 1970s, he found few takers. After the dual shocks of Nixon's August 1971 order severing the remaining link between the dollar and gold, and Kissinger's 1973 oil hoax, Wall Street was looking for stability, and the major investment firms were quite conservative in their investments.

The 1976 election of Jimmy Carter, however, initiated a process of economic degeneration that led to many changes in how Wall Street conducted its business, changes which cleared the way for Milken and his allies to unleash their financial experiments on the nation.

Already, the stage had been set by the mid-1970s'

Kissinger-engineered oil hoax, which led to skyrocketing petroleum prices and a flood of what came to be known as "petro-dollars" into the American banking system. The "petro-dollars" of the seventies paved the way for the narco-dollar invasion of the 1980s.

The appointment of Paul Volcker as chairman of the Federal Reserve Board in 1979 was a watershed in the process of opening the U.S. economy for wholesale looting. Volcker raised interest rates to the highest sustained levels in U.S. history. These high interest rates squeezed bank profits even further, as the cost of borrowing money from the Fed went through the roof.

The only solution to this crisis, most bankers concluded, was to deregulate the banking system and thereby transform it into the newest safe haven for illegal cash. By the time Congress passed the Garn-St Germain Act in 1982, the U.S. banking system had been completely opened to foreign flight capital, and banks and savings and loan institutions (S&Ls) were given the green light for the first time ever to invest directly in real estate, junk bonds, and many other speculative ventures which had been previously prohibited.

One big advocate of total deregulation was then-Vice President George Bush, who was the chairman of President Reagan's blue ribbon task force on deregulation. Under his and Volcker's direction, most antitrust legislation was struck down, thus allowing the huge mergers and takeovers of the 1980s to occur, with funds raised by Milken's networks.

Milken and Junk Bonds

With Volcker at the Fed running interference for the drug bankers, and with deregulators in the Executive

Branch striking down protective regulations in conjunc-
tion with their congressional allies, the doors were
opened for bringing the offshore drug profits back into
the United States.

And it was Michael Milken and his domination over
the junk bond market which provided the mechanism
by which the funds would be laundered.

Junk bonds offered an ideal way to repatriate drug
money and other illicit funds. From his promotion of
junk bonds in the mid-1970s, Milken built up a network
of "corporate raiders" around him, many of whom had
organized crime connections. They had excess dollars,
money which they used initially to buy real estate, restau-
rants, casinos, and other cash-based businesses ideally
suited for washing money. However, as the drug trade
flourished, these traditional means of laundering money
became inadequate. They needed bigger, more expensive targets.

Again, it was Milken who provided these targets.
During a brainstorming session with the brass at Drexel
Burnham, Milken won over CEO Fred Joseph to the idea
of using junk bonds to fund corporate takeovers. The
same raiders who had been purchasing junk bonds could
use their money to take over large corporations, especially corporations with a large cash flow, such as food,
beverage, and tobacco companies. Milken would sell
junk bonds to part of his network of raiders, who would
use their illicit funds to purchase the junk bonds. The
money raised from the sale of the junk bonds would
provide the funds for another raider to buy the company.
Then, the new owner could mix in (i.e., launder) further
drug revenues with the cash flow of his newly purchased
company.

One assistant U.S. attorney who has been building cases against money laundering for years, said that this process makes it very difficult to trace the initial funds. "To start with," he said, "these transactions [the takeovers] are very difficult to follow. But when you start using companies with heavy cash flows, which are ideal for money laundering, it becomes almost impossible."

U.S. tax laws also favored use of junk bond sales for takeovers. Under provisions of the corporate tax code, interest paid on debt is deductible, while dividends received from stock holdings are not. The tax laws favor those raiders who take over firms through generating huge debt responsibilities, while penalizing those who act to increase profits through investments which increase productivity.

Huge tax liabilities were thus evaded through the debt-backed takeovers financed through junk bonds. In addition to his network of raiders, who to a man enjoyed long-term relationships with the ADL, Milken's operation could not have succeeded without the aid of the finest lawyers dirty money could buy. While there were many firms which offered their help, three stand out and all three are deep into the ADL circuit:

• *Paul, Weiss, Rifkind, Wharton and Garrison.* Founder Seymour Rifkind served as an adviser to one of Milken's leading raiders, Ronald Perelman. Rifkind was counsel to the Golding family, which Perelman married into. The grandfather of Perelman's first wife Faith Golding, was a founder of the ADL's Sterling National Bank. Rifkind joined the board of Perelman's company MacAndrew & Forbes, which he used as a vehicle to take over Pantry Pride and Revlon, two of the country's largest consumer-goods outfits.

Rifkind was also on the board of Revlon, even while it was being targeted by Perelman. Rifkind protégé Arthur Liman would serve on Milken's defense team following his 1989 indictment for insider trading. Liman joined the Milken team fresh from a stint as chief counsel to the House of Representatives' Iran-Contra panel, in which capacity he helped cover up the ADL's pivotal role in that covert criminal program.

• *Skadden Arps, Slate, Meagher and Flom.* Senior partner Joseph Flom has been at the center of every major takeover during the 1970s and 1980s. According to Connie Bruck, author of *Predator's Ball,* and a leading expert on takeovers, Flom and Martin Lipton of Wachtell, Lipton "virtually had created the takeover business in the seventies." Anyone looking for a takeover target hired either Flom or Lipton; those firms which became targets would hire the other one for "protection."

According to one prosecutor who worked on the Wall Street fraud cases in the late 1980s, "these two law firms were just like the 'insurance business' run by the mob—if you don't get insurance by hiring one of them, you might get targeted." Mob lawyer and former ADL National Chairman Kenneth Bialkin joined Skadden Arps in 1988.

• *Wachtell, Lipton.*

Milken's Monsters

Once George Bush's task force eliminated the regulatory measures which had protected American enterprises and corporations from sharks and looters, and with teams of lawyers in place to defend them, it was time for Milken to unleash his raiders.

During the decade of the 1980s, more than $1.5 trillion was diverted into corporate takeovers and leveraged buyouts (LBOs). Of this amount, more than $60 billion went directly into the pockets of the investment bankers, the "dealmakers" (i.e., the "raiders"), and their attorneys.

Henry Kravis, one of the leading dealmakers of the 1980s, exploited his close ADL ties to raise money for the takeover antics of his firm, Kohlberg Kravis & Roberts (KKR). Once Drexel Burnham decided to use junk bonds to finance takeovers, the Kravis-Milken connection was a natural.

Milken and his raider networks provided billions of dollars to help finance KKR's takeovers. Henry Kravis' KKR was created in 1976 with $120,000. By 1990, it had borrowed $58 billion from banks, S&Ls, insurance companies and pension funds, to take over more than 35 companies. While cousins Henry Kravis and George Roberts are now worth more than $500 million each, the firms they took over have been loaded up with debt, threatening the investments made by S&Ls, insurance companies, and pension funds.

To pay this debt, the firms were asset-stripped, and forced to close down factories, throwing hundreds of thousands of people onto unemployment lines. Many of these deals resulted in bankruptcies, forcing the federal government to cover the losses when the bankrupted firm was taken over, by borrowing from a federally insured bank, S&L or pension fund.

While the new management created by the takeover was dismantling the company to pay the debt generated to buy it, the raiders came away with huge profits. Milken alone received a $550 million bonus from Drexel in 1986, and he doled out another $150 million in bonuses to his team.

Working hand in hand with Milken in the looting of America were a collection of figures with close links to both organized crime and the ADL. Collectively, they were given the name "Milken's Monsters" by one of their most notorious members, Meshulam Riklis. Riklis, the front man for the ADL's "Minneapolis Mafia," had been the middle-man in the Vesco-Bialkin takeover of Investors Overseas Service.

The Monsters were Milken's first followers, those who saw in his promotion of junk bonds the means by which they could launder funds, while simultaneously generating the leverage to take over major corporations, which would further facilitate their laundering. Many of them began by purchasing insurance companies, which in turn became major purchasers of junk bonds. In the early stages of Milken's ascendancy, the Monsters routinely passed funds back and forth among themselves, buying issues of junk bonds offered by each other's insurance companies. This first group of Monsters included:

• *Carl Lindner,* who took over Cincinnati's Provident Bank in 1966. He then acquired Great American, a property and casualty insurance company, which operated as a subsidiary of the financial holding company American Financial Corp. In 1974, when Lindner was just beginning his relationship with Milken, he was under investigation by the Securities and Exchange Commission (SEC) for violating anti-fraud and anti-manipulation regulations.

We have already encountered Lindner as the United Brands owner who joined with Edmund Safra in staking out the biggest claims in Amex. Lindner and his "Purple Gang" partner Max Fisher literally took over United Brands over the dead body of CEO Eli Black, who mysteriously fell or jumped out of a window of the Pan Am building in New York City, while in the midst of fighting the Lindner grab.

Black's son, Leon Black, was placated by a lucrative job as one of Milken's top allies, as a "strategic planner" at Drexel. It was Leon Black who in 1979 helped Milken convince Drexel CEO Fred Joseph that Drexel should use its clout from junk bonds to back the raiders in takeovers. Black said the raiders are the "robber barons of the future. . . . [T]hese are the guys who are building empires."

Lindner soon became Drexel's biggest client, in both trading and corporate finance. He was represented by Peter Fishbein of Kaye, Scholer, a law firm which serves as official outside counsel to the ADL's Sterling Bank. Fishbein has been an ADL officer since 1970. In 1992, federal regulators banned Fishbein from ever having any dealings with banks or any other financial institutions, as the result of a probe that linked him and the law firm to a coverup of S&L looting by Lincoln Savings and Loan's Charles Keating.

• *Saul Steinberg,* who started a computer leasing business, Leasco, in 1961, shortly after graduation from college. He was backed up in his early takeovers by Sanford Weill, a leader of Wall Street's "New Crowd" who was named ADL's Man of the Year in 1981. Weill's lawyer at the time was the ADL's next national chairman, Kenneth Bialkin. With Weill's backing, Steinberg took over Reliance Insurance Co., which he used to make a play for New York's Chemical Bank in 1969.

After taking over Reliance, Steinberg brought in Bial-kin's law firm, Willkie, Farr and Gallagher to represent it. The Saul Steinberg Foundation is also represented by Bialkin's firm. It donates heavily to the ADL.

• *Meshulam Riklis,* who spent much of the 1970s under investigation by the SEC and U.S. Customs Service narcotics officials. Riklis used Rapid American, a con-glomerate which included International Playtex, Schen-ley Industries, Lerner Shops, and RKO-Stanley Warner Theatres, to finance his raids.

Shortly after Riklis took Rapid American private, Lindner and Steinberg followed suit, with American Fi-nancial and Reliance respectively. The Riklis Family Foundation has contributed heavily to the ADL, ac-cording to Internal Revenue Service (IRS) documents.

• *Laurence Tisch,* whose insurance company CNA was a frequent investor in junk bonds issued by Milken. His Tisch Foundation has provided funds for the ADL.

Lindner, Steinberg, Riklis, and Tisch all invested heavily in each other's offerings. For example, Carl Lind-ner, through American Financial, was the second largest shareholder in Steinberg's Reliance and in Tisch's Loews Corp., as well as a major shareholder in Riklis' Rapid American. When Milken needed to raise funds, any one of these four could be counted on for quick bucks.

The Monsters Unleashed

There were others from the same organized crime net-works who joined the Monsters. Victor Posner, who operates out of rundown offices in Miami Beach, made a fortune in real estate in the 1930s and 1940s. Like many of the oldtimers in the Milken-ADL stable, he, too, was reputed to have been a financial partner of Meyer Lansky.

Posner, who like Meshulam Riklis engaged in "creative financing" before hooking up with Milken, was forced to sign a consent decree with the SEC over allegations that he misused pension funds from Sharon Steel, a firm he looted in the 1970s.

Ronald Perelman, another of Milken's raiders, has deep ties to the ADL. Perelman married Faith Golding, whose grandfather founded Sterling National Bank. Mac-Andrews & Forbes was the vehicle used by Perelman to take over Pantry Pride, with financing from Milken. He then used Pantry Pride to take over Revlon, financed again by Milken, and advised by Skadden Arps' Joe Flom.

With the same network of advisers and some inside political help, Perelman was able to take advantage of the S&L asset giveaway known as the Southwest Plan, in which he received the assets of six shut down Texas S&Ls for a nominal fee, while receiving a $900 million tax credit to cut his liabilities from the Revlon takeover. When Perelman divorced Golding, his lawyer was mob attorney Roy Cohn.

Up until he died of AIDS in the late 1980s, Cohn maintained intimate, behind the scenes ties to the ADL. According to internal ADL documents, Cohn was never placed on the League's directorate out of fear that the ADL would lose the financial backing of many prominent ex-Communists, who still detested Cohn for his antics during the 1950s Joe McCarthy Red Purges.

Another of Milken's raiders was Nelson Peltz, who bankrupted his family's frozen food business and was personally close to bankruptcy when he obtained Milken's backing to take a 9.5% share of Sterling Bancorp in 1980. Next, Milken helped Peltz and partner Peter May with a takeover of Triangle Industries, which they then used to leverage a $456 million bid for National Can, financed completely by junk bond sales by Milken.

In these cases, and hundreds more, Milken provided the financing by which the raiders took over corporate America. With almost unlimited funds, Milken bragged to an associate, "We're going to tee-up GM, Ford, and IBM. And make them cringe."

Milken's confidence came from the knowledge that behind all his investment wizardry stood a pool of nearly $6.25 trillion—the gross profits of the international dope trade from 1978-1990. Milken never owned up to his sources of capital. At the peak of his power, he would simply dash off "highly confident letters" informing take-over targets that he would be able to generate whatever amount of liquidity would be needed to buy out their companies.

Milken's other source of confidence was his deep connection to the ADL. Milken believed that by pouring money into the League's coffers, he would be forever "untouchable."

In 1987, for example, the Milken Family Fund gave $28,000 to the ADL Foundation-Christian Rescuers Project, and $10,250 to the ADL Foundation, in addition to a grant to the ADL of $344,000. The same foundation gave the ADL $29,000 in 1990.

The Capital Foundation, also under Milken's control, approved $1.245 million to the ADL for "future payment" in the year ending Nov. 30, 1989.

At a Ku Klux Klan meeting, circa 1915, candidates for membership are received.

5 | Colluding With Terrorists

In December 1985, then-FBI Director William Webster, speaking at the National Press Club in Washington, D.C., admitted that a "Jewish underground" had emerged as a serious terrorist threat to the United States during the preceding twelve months. Indeed, over the course of 1985, the Jewish Defense League (JDL) had been responsible for a string of sophisticated bombings that left two people dead, a dozen others seriously wounded, and caused millions of dollars in property damage.

Alex Odeh, the head of the California branch of the Arab-American Anti-Discrimination Committee (AADC), had been killed when a bomb went off at the group's Santa Ana office. Seven other people were hospitalized in the attack. Tscherim Soobzokov, a victim of the Justice

Department's Nazi-hunting Office of Special Investigations (OSI), had also died when a booby trap bomb blew up his home in Paterson, N.J. A Boston police officer, responding to a JDL bomb threat at the local office of AADC, was crippled for life when a pipe bomb blew up as he was attempting to defuse it.

In each of these instances, the bomb attacks had been preceded by noisy public demonstrations and inflammatory press statements by Mordechai Levy, the leader of a JDL splinter group, the Jewish Defense Organization (JDO).

Although FBI boss Webster left his National Press Club audience with the impression that the so-called "Jewish underground" was a mysterious and amorphous outfit about which the FBI had little information, in truth, the Bureau had an exhaustive profile of the key personnel and their mode of operation. FBI agents on the scene of the Santa Ana, Calif. murder of Alex Odeh knew the identities of the three men who planted the bomb before Odeh's body was even removed from the murder scene. The killers were longtime JDL members Andy Green, Keith Fuchs and Bob Manning. The American-born trio were residents of an Israeli kibbutz in the occupied territories called Kiryat Arba. Kiryat Arba was a training camp and safehouse for the JDL and its Israeli affiliate, the Kach Party.

The FBI listed Fuchs, Green and Manning as suspects in a total of 25 terrorist attacks inside the United States. Fuchs had been jailed in Israel in 1983 for firing a Soviet-made AK-47 rifle at a busload of Arabs on the West Bank. Manning had served time in jail in the United States for bombing the home of an Arab-American activist. When the three JDLers arrived in Los Angeles several days before the Odeh murder, they were already under FBI surveillance.

It's no wonder that FBI Director Webster was not anxious to discuss details with the room full of reporters at the National Press Club. The Bureau had been in a position to prevent the bombing of the Santa Ana AADC office and they had flubbed it.

Or worse?

At the same time that the "Jewish underground" was conducting its bombing spree from coast to coast, the FBI was relying increasingly on the ADL for information about extremist groups! This was the same ADL that would join with the KGB and the East German Stasi in covering the trail of the assassins of Sweden's head of state, Olof Palme.

Even more to the point, this was the same ADL that was instrumental in the creation and deployment of such diverse terrorist groups as the JDL and the Ku Klux Klan!

According to Robert Friedman, the biographer of JDL founder Rabbi Meir Kahane, the militant Jewish group was controlled from its founding days by a secret three-person committee made up of future Israeli Prime Minister and Mossad operations chief Yitzhak Shamir, right-wing Israeli parliamentarian Geula Cohen, and Brooklyn ADL Chairman Bernard Deutch.

It was at a December 1969 meeting between Cohen and Kahane, arranged by Deutch, that the JDL launched its campaign of terror and intimidation against Soviet diplomats in New York and Washington, aimed at forcing the Soviets to loosen up their emigration laws for Jews. In the early days, before JDL head Kahane hooked up with mobster Joe Colombo, and many JDLers began funding their terrorist operations by selling dope or running

syndicate shakedown operations, ADL man Deutch had
been the moneybags behind the Jewish militants.
Deutch's involvement with the JDL was such a well-kept
secret that his Kahane links remained virtually unknown
until 1991.

Just as the B'nai B'rith had quietly steered other
Jewish-American groups to smuggle arms into Russia on
the eve of the Bolshevik Revolution, the ADL ran the
"Jewish underground" from behind the scenes, often
going through the motions of publicly denouncing the
JDL violence to make sure that no direct links were ever
surfaced.

ADL's 'Ku Klutz Klanners'

Mordechai Levy, the leader of the JDL splinter group that
managed to show up on the doorsteps of Alex Odeh and
Tscherim Soobzokov on the eves of their assassinations,
maintained direct and frequent contact with the ADL's
Fact Finding Division head, Irwin Suall. Just two weeks
before the AADC's Washington, D.C. office was blown
up on Nov. 29, 1985, Levy had appeared as the featured
speaker at a press conference hosted by the Federation
of Jewish Organizations of Greater Washington, an um-
brella group led by both the ADL and B'nai B'rith, to
present a list of "enemies of the Jewish people." AADC
was among the groups listed.

On more than one occasion, Levy's *provocateur*
antics nearly exposed the ADL's hand in fomenting domestic violence.

On Feb. 16, 1979, Levy, using the pseudonym
"James Guttman," filed an application with the U.S. Park
Service in Philadelphia, Pa. to obtain permission to hold

a rally. The rally permit sought by Levy/Guttman was not filed in the name of the JDL. Levy was posing as a leader of the American Nazi Party, seeking a permit for a Ku Klux Klan and Nazi Party rally at Independence Hall, the site of the signing of the Declaration of Independence.

According to the rally permit, Levy was planning a "white power rally, to show white masses unity of white race, and to show the world niggers and Jews are cowards." Among the paraphernalia Levy listed on the application were: "swastikas, banners, Nazi uniforms, KKK paraphernalia ... will burn cross, swastika picket signs saying 'Hitler was right—gas commie Jews.'"

Working out of the Philadelphia offices of the Jewish Defense League, Levy organized local chapters of the KKK and neo-Nazi groups to attend the Independence Hall rally. In the case of the Trenton, N.J. KKK, Levy had an inside track. James Rosenberg, also known as "Jimmy Mitchell" and "Jimmy Anderson"—a full-time paid employee of the ADL Fact Finding Division—had successfully infiltrated the local chapter of the Klan.

Rosenberg had recently attempted unsuccessfully to get some of the local KKKers to blow up the Trenton headquarters of the National Association for the Advancement of Colored People (NAACP). At the same time he was posing as "James Guttman," neo-Nazi, Levy was also mobilizing the Jewish community and every ragtag left-wing radical group in the greater Philadelphia area to attend a mass demonstration "to confront" the KKK and Nazis at Independence Hall. All the ingredients were there for a serious riot—courtesy of the ADL.

Fortunately, word of Levy's scam on the Park Service leaked out to the Philadelphia press. After one Philadelphia newspaper ran a banner headline "Nazi Rally-Rouser Really Jewish," the Park Service yanked the permit. Levy's ADL handlers ordered him to lay low for a while.

After all, there was no need to jeopardize Levy or even Rosenberg's standing as professional *agents provocateur* inside the racist right-wing. The ADL had plenty of other aces up their sleeves, and not all of them were Jewish infiltrators.

Goodman, Cheney, Schwerner— and the ADL

One of the most shocking instances of racist violence during the civil rights battles in the South of the U.S. during the 1960s was the execution-style murders of three civil rights workers in Philadelphia, Miss. in 1964. The murders of Andrew Goodman, Robert Cheney and Mitchell Schwerner sent shock waves across America and the world, as many people began to realize for the first time that the Confederacy, far from being dead, was very much alive and very much committed to rolling back the tide of equal rights for all races—at least in the Deep South.

True to its historical roots in the Southern Jurisdiction of the Scottish Rite Freemasonry and in the original Confederate secessionist plot, the ADL—contrary to its own published propaganda—lined up squarely with the Klan where it counted the most: with its checkbook.

One particularly sordid instance of collusion between the ADL and the KKK came to light in a hail of bullets on the night of June 30, 1968 in Meridian, Miss., outside the home of ADL official Meyer Davidson.

When the smoke cleared, a local schoolteacher named Kathy Ainsworth lay dead, and a second man,

Thomas A. Terrants III, lay dying after being hit with over 70 bullets fired by 22 local police and FBI agents. Miraculously, Terrants survived the attack.

Terrants and Ainsworth, both local Klan members, had been set up. They went to Davidson's home that night to plant a bomb on his doorstep, not knowing that the leader of their own KKK chapter had betrayed them, and that a small army of police and FBI sharpshooters was waiting in the bushes to ambush them.

The entire affair had been staged by the ADL. The *agent provocateur* inside the local KKK chapter who set up Terrants and Ainsworth was one of the killers of Goodman, Cheney and Schwerner. Alton Wayne Roberts was out on bail awaiting his trial, along with six other members of the White Knights of the Ku Klux Klan, for the Philadelphia, Miss. murders when, in the early spring of 1968, he cut a deal with the ADL's regional director, Adolph Botnick. The New Orleans-based Botnick had been a longstanding friend of the late Guy Bannister, the former FBI special agent implicated by District Attorney Jim Garrison in the assassination of President John F. Kennedy.

Botnick, with the blessings of Meridian-based FBI Special Agent Frank Watts and Meridian police detective Luke Scarborough, agreed to pay Alton Wayne Roberts and his brother Raymond Roberts $69,000 to become the League's paid *agents provocateur.* $25,000 in unmarked twenty-dollar bills was hand-delivered from New Orleans to the Roberts brothers just days before the Ainsworth-Terrants ambush.

At the time the deal was struck, the White Knights, led by the two Roberts brothers, had been on a ninemonth bombing spree. The brothers were prime sus-

pects in ten separate acts of racist violence, in addition
to the Philadelphia murders. Three of these attacks were
directed against synagogues and Jewish leaders in Missis-
sippi.

The Roberts brothers, as per their deal with Botnick,
ordered two of their Klan underlings to deliver the bomb
to Davidson's home. They then tipped off the FBI and
the local police about the exact time the attack would
occur.

In return for their continuing services to the ADL
after the Davidson incident, the brothers were given slap
on the wrist sentences and placed in the FBI's witness
protection program. For his part in the Goodman,
Cheney and Schwerner murders, Alton Wayne Roberts
spent less than three years in jail.

The Meridian incident was classic ADL. The League
used the "racist attack" against Meyer Davidson as a scare
tactic fundraising ploy. The money they raised more than
covered the costs of buying up the two KKKers as their
permanent *agents provocateur* inside the Klan. The
League parlayed their financing of the Roberts brothers
into an ever-closer relationship with the FBI, which was
delighted to have the ADL finance and deploy two of the
Klan's most violent terrorists.

EIRNS/Carlos de Hoyos

Whiskey baron Edgar Bronfman, the ADL's "friend of Moscow."

6 In Bed With Communist Dictators and Spies

On the day in November 1985 that Israeli spy Jonathan Jay Pollard was arrested, things went haywire at the ADL's headquarters near United Nations Plaza in New York City. National Chairman Kenneth Bialkin immediately flew off to Israel to assess the damage and to make arrangements for the appropriate American attorneys to be brought in to represent not only the jailed spy, but the other, more senior players in the nominally Israeli spy ring.

Among the most important of those senior players was Col. Aviem Sella, an Israeli Air Force war hero who had been Pollard's recruiter on behalf of the secret Israeli techno-spy unit, Lekem.

Sella's cover for his spy recruiting was that he was in the United States taking graduate courses at New York

University; and Sella's wife Ruth, a practicing attorney, reportedly was working on the staff of the ADL's legal department while the couple lived in New York.

Any published links between the ADL and the Pollard spy apparatus could naturally prove very damaging, especially in light of the cozy relationship the League was enjoying with the Reagan White House at the time.

While still in Israel, Bialkin telephoned fellow ADL man Leonard Garment of the politically powerful law firm of Dickstein, Shapiro. Garment was then the personal lawyer for U.S. Attorney General Edwin Meese. He agreed at Bialkin's urging to represent Sella in the Pollard matter, despite the obvious, severe conflict of interest.

At the ADL's Washington, D.C. office, Mira Lansky Boland was also undoubtedly worried that her own links to Pollard might surface. Lansky Boland had been a classmate and pal of Pollard at the graduate school program in national security affairs at the Fletcher School of Diplomacy of Tufts University in Cambridge, Mass. Upon graduation in 1978, both Lansky and Pollard had been immediately placed into sensitive posts in the U.S. intelligence community. Pollard had gone into Naval intelligence and had almost immediately begun funneling secrets to Israel.

Lansky Boland had gone to work for the Central Intelligence Agency. After a two-year stint with the CIA, she had transferred to the Pentagon, where she worked under Dr. Andrew Marshall at the Office of Net Assessments, a little known but powerful unit that prepared technical assessments of Soviet military capabilities. In 1982, Lansky had left the government to work full-time for the ADL in Washington.

Shortly after her arrival at the ADL from the Pentagon, she was assigned as the case officer on the League's multi-million dollar campaign to smear and jail Lyndon LaRouche and scores of his associates.

Following the Pollard arrest, Andrew Marshall would be identified as a suspected senior member of the Pollard spy ring, although no charges were ever brought against him and he remains to this day in his post at the Defense Department. To this day, Pentagon officials have never succeeded in pinning down the identity of the "Mr. X" who gave Pollard the code numbers of the classified documents that the Naval intelligence analyst then stole and passed on to Lekem.

Both Pollard and Lansky had gotten their government spy jobs courtesy of Fletcher School professor Uri Ra'anan. Ra'anan, an Oxford University-trained Middle East expert, had himself been an Israeli government intelligence operative, posted in New York City and Washington during the 1950s and 1960s. While serving as a "press attaché" at the Israeli embassy in Washington in the mid-1960s, Ra'anan had helped set up a unit that would recruit Israeli spies from the ranks of American businessmen traveling frequently to the Soviet Union and Eastern Europe.

That spy unit, which was unearthed in a series of civil suits beginning in 1967, was housed at the headquarters of the B'nai B'rith International. Ra'anan's contact point inside the B'nai B'rith was Philip Klutznick, an honorary national chairman of the ADL who would later serve as President Jimmy Carter's secretary of commerce.

Among the damage control efforts launched by the ADL in the wake of the Pollard arrest was the planting of a string of news accounts and editorials portraying Pollard as a loyal American who was also committed to the security of the state of Israel. Harmless, "friendly espionage" was the term coined by the League and its small army of paid agents inside the news media.

Unfortunately, Pollard's spying was anything but harmless or friendly.

The Lekem unit, headed by the former chief of European operations for the Mossad, Rafael ("Dirty Rafi") Eytan, was passing on the most sensitive of the American national security secrets heisted by Pollard to the Soviet KGB. In return, Moscow was opening up the pipeline of Soviet Jews to Israel.

It was treachery of the highest order, and then-Secretary of Defense Caspar Weinberger was fully aware of the magnitude of Pollard's crimes when he asked the judge to sentence Pollard to life in prison after the spy agreed to plead guilty. In a 46-page, classified affidavit submitted to the judge in the Pollard case, Weinberger showed that much of the Pollard material wound up in Soviet hands, and that it would cost the United States billions of dollars to repair the national security damage done by the Pollard spy ring.

In fact, of the millions of pages of classified documents funneled by Pollard to the KGB, a majority were of no critical interest to Israel at all.

Whiskey for the Red Dictators

Did Kenneth Bialkin or Mira Lansky Boland, or any of the other ADL officials who abetted Pollard in his spy work, know that the pilfered material was going to the KGB? The answer to that question has never been made public. To this day, only the players in the espionage operation know for sure.

However, it is unquestionably the case that at the same time the ADL was knee-deep in the Pollard stew, top ADL officials were working hand in glove with the Soviet bloc intelligence services on several other projects that would have devastating consequences for the United States.

One such ADL "friend of Moscow" was whiskey baron Edgar Bronfman.

The third-generation Bronfmans had successfully transformed their fathers' Prohibition-era bootlegging business into a "legit" whiskey empire, Seagram's. This transformation had been aided early on by the U.S. Treasury Department, which cut a deal with Sam and Abe Bronfman at the close of Prohibition, enabling them to pay several million dollars in "back taxes" in return for a whitewashing of their decade of big-time crimes.

The Bronfman family came out of the deal as multimillionaires—with all their ties to the Lansky syndicate still intact.

Abner "Longie" Zwillman was not the only Prohibition-era gangster who profited from the old saw, "from rags to rackets to riches to respectability." By the 1950s, the Bronfmans' image had been so cleaned up that Edgar could marry into the "Our Crowd" Loeb family, and his sister Phyllis could marry Jean Lambert of the Belgian branch of the Rothschild clan. The Lambert family was the European connection in Drexel Burnham Lambert.

However, image-polishing is one thing. Reality is another. As late as 1972, the Montreal, Canada Crime Commission had issued a report naming Mitchell Bronfman as a crime partner of one of the city's biggest gangsters, Willy Obront. The pair were implicated in dope smuggling. Willy and Mitchell owned a nightspot in the middle of Meyer Lansky's turf in North Miami called the Pagoda North, which was a favorite hangout for Vito Genovese and other big-time hoodlums.

Edgar Bronfman, for his part, sought out some very peculiar clientele for his family's whiskey business. In 1986, as the Pollard affair was playing out, one of Edgar Bronfman's assistants at the World Jewish Congress (Bronfman had taken over the WJC and turned it into an international arm of the ADL, on whose National Commission he sits) established ties to the brutal Communist regime in East Germany. Bronfman's Seagram's was made the exclusive distributor of booze to East Germany's ruling SED (Communist Party).

In 1988, Edgar Bronfman himself traveled to East Berlin where he was the guest of honor of SED boss Erich Honecker and top party official Hermann Axen. On that trip, Bronfman vowed that he would personally arrange for the East German leader to make a state visit to Washington, D.C. to meet with President Ronald Reagan.

Even one year later, with the Berlin Wall and East German Communism about to collapse, Edgar Bronfman was back in East Germany again, this time promising to marshal the resources of the World Jewish Congress and the ADL to block the reunification of Germany, which he dubbed a "sellout of socialism." In return for those efforts, Bronfman was given the highest civilian award offered by East Germany, the "People's Friendship Medal in Gold."

Edgar's brother and business partner Charles was also a true friend of the Honecker dictatorship. As the head of the Canadian-East German Friendship Society, he was able to control all passports and visas between the two countries.

But there was much more to the Bronfman-East Germany liaison than a lucrative whiskey contract and a few medals.

The Palme Affair

On Feb. 28, 1986, Swedish Prime Minister Olof Palme was assassinated by a lone gunman on the streets of Stockholm. Just before his assassination, Palme was in the process of cracking down on Swedish arms dealers who were funneling guns to the Nicaraguan Contras and to the Iranian regime. The Iran-Contra scandal had not yet broken publicly and Palme's probe threatened to blow the lid on the entire covert program. Curiously, many of the guns being sold by the Swedes—with the collusion of Oliver North, CIA chief William Casey and the Israelis—were coming from East Germany and other Soviet bloc states.

Was Palme in the process of unearthing a cynical East-West collusion, an even nastier reality buried beneath the then-unknown Irangate scandal? Had he inadvertently stumbled onto the trail of the ADL's own involvement in this demimonde of gun and drug dealing?

The answer to that question was at least implicitly given within days of the Palme assassination, when the ADL joined with the KGB and the East German Stasi (state security service) in an effort to blame the Palme murder on Swedish associates of Lyndon LaRouche. ADL Fact Finding Division chief Irwin Suall, himself an Oxford University-trained active member of the Socialist International, personally flew to Stockholm to fuel the disinformation campaign linking LaRouche to the Palme murder.

Soviet Ambassador Boris Pankin, a major general in

the KGB who specialized in planting disinformation in the Western press, directed the Soviet side of the "LaRouche killed Palme" hoax, while Georgii Arbatov, the head of the Soviet Academy of Science's U.S.A.-Canada Institute, added his voice to those accusing LaRouche. Ultimately, the Soviet government-owned TV network aired an hour-long "docudrama" elaborating the LaRouche lie.

The role of Edgar Bronfman's pals in the East German Stasi in the Palme coverup would not surface until three years later. However, back in August 1989, the Stockholm daily newspaper *Expressen* revealed that Swedish police had bugged the home of a resident KGB agent and had audiotape evidence that the man knew at least 24 hours before Palme's murder that the Prime Minister would be killed.

The pivotal role of the Stasi in the Palme murder coverup was first revealed in the Aug. 20-26, 1992 edition of *Journalisten,* the magazine of the Swedish Journalists Association, which published an interview with a former top Stasi officer named Herbert Brehmer. In that interview and in a series of subsequent Swedish nationwide radio broadcasts, Brehmer confessed that as an official of Department X (disinformation) of the Stasi, he had engineered the disinformation campaign blaming the European Labor Party (ELP), the Scandinavian affiliates of Lyndon LaRouche, for the Palme murder.

Brehmer told *Journalisten:*

"At my desk I drew up the outlines of how the ELP theory would be conduited into the Swedish police investigation. The plan was to have a national Swedish newspaper receive an anonymous telephone tip-off. . . . As an alternative, the information would go directly to one of the special tip-off phones made available by the police. The content would be along the lines that the caller 'knew that the ELP had committed the crime.' In addition, he or she had 'witnessed hectic activity in the ELP headquarters in the night.' Nothing was really true, but it sounded well-informed and credible."

Indeed. The 1986 Stasi-manufactured disinformation was conduited into the U.S. media through the ADL. NBC-TV ran the story as a leading news item on their evening news broadcast, interviewing ADL official Suall as part of their coverage. Ultimately, the U.S. Justice Department would use the Palme disinformation to justify a massive paramilitary police raid against LaRouche's home and offices of his associates in Leesburg, Va. in October 1986.

The ADL and the OSI

The "LaRouche killed Palme" hoax was no isolated instance of Edgar Bronfman and the ADL teaming up with a Communist secret police agency to target a political enemy or ply a lucrative business scam. It was standard operating procedure.

According to syndicated columnists Rowland Evans and Robert Novak, on Jan. 23, 1989 Bronfman hosted a secret meeting at his New York City penthouse to forge what the columnists dubbed a "Jews for grain" deal between the Soviet Union and Israel. Also present at the gathering was Dwayne Andreas, the chairman of the Archer Daniels Midland (ADM) grain cartel, and a longstanding ally and financial backer of the ADL. The *Wall Street Journal* had dubbed Andreas "Gorbachov's closest pal in the West." At congressional hearings, Andreas identified former ADL National Chairman Ben Epstein as the man who taught him all he knew about politics.

The Bronfman-Andreas deal was straightforward: In return for vast quantities of dirt-cheap grain from ADM and other U.S.-based grain cartels, the Soviet government would permit the mass exodus of Soviet Jews to Israel.

It was an updated version of the Pollard espionage affair, in which U.S. military secrets were swapped for controlled Soviet Jewish migration to Israel. The invariant in the two efforts was the central role of the ADL.

As part of the Bronfman-Andreas deal, the Soviet KGB teamed up with the ADL and Bronfman's World Jewish Congress (WJC) to foment a diplomatic breach between the Reagan administration and Austrian President Kurt Waldheim, the former secretary general of the United Nations. The KGB manufactured and the ADL-WJC conduited phony evidence that Waldheim had been a top Nazi war criminal during World War II. U.S. Attorney General Ed Meese, still employing the legal services of ADL fellow traveler Leonard Garment, bit on the forged material and declared Waldheim *persona non grata* in the United States.

The purpose of the smear job was to shut down Austria as a way-station for Soviet Jews coming out into the West. In the past, once Soviet Jews landed on Austrian soil, they were granted political refugee status, which then enabled them to settle in any country of their choosing. The majority either stayed in Western Europe or found their way to the United States. Very few went to Israel voluntarily. With Austria shut down, Bronfman and Gorbachov worked out alternative routes through Warsaw Pact states and eventually set up direct flights from the Soviet Union to Israel, to ensure that the Soviet refugees had no choice as to where they would live.

By the time Bronfman and Andreas forged their "Jews for grain" deal with Gorbachov in early 1989, the ADL had just about perfected their use of forged KGB documents to smear the entire Eastern European community in the United States as closet wartime Nazis.

As early as 1979, the ADL had played a pivotal role in getting legislation through the U.S. Congress establishing the Office of Special Investigations (OSI), a special Nazi-hunting unit inside the Criminal Division of the Justice Department. ADL asset Rep. Elizabeth Holtzman had sponsored the bill, which effectively stripped naturalized American citizens of Central European and Ukrainian descent of their constitutional rights by providing for automatic denaturalization and deportation without due process, if the OSI could produce evidence that they had been tied to the Nazis during World War II.

And where did the lion's share of this evidence come from, 40 years after the end of World War II? From the Soviet archives!

The ADL-sponsored OSI provided Moscow with a foot in the door to the American judicial system. For the first time ever, Soviet documents and witnesses were given full standing in U.S. court proceedings, no questions asked. While a handful of the people targeted by the ADL-OSI may have been low-level Nazi sympathizers or assets during the war, many innocent people fell victim to the KGB's sophisticated forgers, courtesy of the ADL and their friends at the Justice Department's OSI:

• *Karl Linnas,* falsely accused of Nazi collaboration, was stripped of his American citizenship and shipped off to the Soviet Union, where he died in a prison, reportedly from a heart attack.

• *Tscherim Soobzokov,* accused of working with the Nazis in his native Belorussia, beat the OSI and even won a lucrative out-of-court libel suit against the *New York Times.* He was then murdered by a Jewish Defense League bomb attack on his Paterson, N.J. home in 1985.

• *Dr. Arthur Rudolph,* a celebrated German-American rocket scientist who contributed greatly to America's space program, was falsely accused by the ADL and OSI of torturing Jews at the Peenemünde research facility in wartime Germany. Rather than lose his lifetime pension with the National Aeronautics and Space Administration (NASA) and throw his family into poverty, he renounced his U.S. citizenship and returned to West Germany. After a three-year probe based on the same evidence passed on by the East German and Soviet authorities to the OSI, West German prosecutors concluded that there was no evidence against Dr. Rudolph.

• *John Demjanjuk,* a Ukrainian-American retired auto worker accused of being the Treblinka concentration camp mass-murderer "Ivan the Terrible," was stripped of his citizenship and hauled off to Israel to stand trial. It was the biggest show trial since the proceedings against Adolph Eichmann, broadcast in its entirety live on Israeli national television. Demjanjuk was convicted and sentenced to death by hanging. Through unflagging efforts by his family and friends, Demjanjuk eventually gathered evidence showing that the OSI had suppressed evidence proving that another man had been identified as the real "Ivan." The case is now pending before both the Israeli Supreme Court and the U.S. Sixth Circuit Court of Appeals in Cincinnati, Ohio.

The ADL's liaison to OSI, Elliot Wells, in a signed letter to the editors of the *Washington Post,* demanded that Demjanjuk not be set free. Using the kind of stilted logic that would make the KGB blush, Wells argued that even if Demjanjuk is innocent of the Treblinka charges, he must be guilty of some other war crimes, and therefore should be held in custody until new evidence can be manufactured.

EIRNS/Philip Ulanowsky

EIRNS/Stuart Lewis

EIRNS/Stuart Lewis

EIRNS/Stuart Lewis

Members of the Get LaRouche Task Force, top left to right: Irwin Suall, Kent Robinson; bottom left to right, Dennis King, Mira Lansky Boland.

7 Railroad!

In early March 1986—within days of the assassination of Sweden's Prime Minister Olof Palme, ADL Fact-Finding department chief Irwin Suall was en route to Stockholm. An Oxford University-trained Fabian Socialist, Suall was the ADL's longtime top dirty trickster. Since 1978, with the publication of the book *Dope, Inc.,* Suall's efforts had been almost obsessively focused against Lyndon LaRouche, the American political economist who had commissioned the anti-drug study published by *EIR.*

Suall's trans-Atlantic voyage to Stockholm was in pursuit of that obsession.

Working in tandem with the East German secret police (Stasi), the Soviet KGB, Swedish socialists and NBC-TV, Suall helped launch the disinformation campaign blaming LaRouche and his Swedish collaborators in the European Labor Party for the Palme assassination.

Just as Suall's efforts were beginning to bear fruit with a series of "LaRouche killed Palme" smear stories in the U.S., Swedish and Soviet press, the ADL trickster was suddenly confronted with a major crisis:

On March 16, 1986, two LaRouche-backed candidates—Mark Fairchild and Janice Hart—won the Illinois Democratic Party primary elections for lieutenant governor and secretary of state, respectively. The LaRouche candidates' victories were no fluke. LaRouche-backed candidates had been winning between 20-40 percent of the vote in Democratic primary elections in different parts of the country since the early 1980s. A leading Democratic Party pollster had written frantic messages to the Illinois state party chairman warning about a LaRouche upset months before the election.

Not surprisingly, the upset victory by the LaRouche slate was electrifying. The Wall Street and Freemasonic circles who own the ADL were shocked into action.

Suall hurried back to New York City where he oversaw the preparation and mass distribution of a violent ADL smear sheet against LaRouche. Over the next few months, according to records of the Federal Election Commission, over 6,000 copies of the ADL libel—at a cost of at least $10,000—were circulated to every member of Congress, 1,580 news outlets and other government offices and opinion makers. Tens of thousands of media attacks against LaRouche—branding him as everything from an anti-Semite, to a KGB agent, to a neo-Nazi to an international terrorist—were published in the United States alone. Among some anti-Zionist lobby and Third World circles, the ADL even accused LaRouche of being a closet "mole" for the Israeli Mossad! The invariant in all the contradictory slanders conjured up by the ADL was to scare people away from the LaRouche political movement.

The ADL smear campaign was a panicked and flagrant violation of its tax-exempt status. It was also a violation of FEC rules, which prohibit a tax-exempt organization from engaging in politicking. On June 16, 1987, the FEC officially acknowledged that the ADL action against LaRouche was illegal; but a few months later, the commissioners decided they would take no action against the League.

The smear campaign was meeting with only modest political success, although it had a severe effect as financial warfare. LaRouche-Democrat candidates continued to do well. In 1988, Claude Jones, a longtime and well-known LaRouche activist, was elected chairman of the Harris County, Texas Democratic Party, shortly after the Illinois victories. Harris County, which includes Houston, is one of the largest electoral districts in the United States, and a Democratic Party stronghold. Jones beat a powerful incumbent to take over the party post.

The *Washington Post* in May 1986—summing up the consensus among the liberal establishment—editorialized that Lyndon LaRouche must be in jail, not on television, by the time of the 1988 presidential elections.

An Already Ongoing Frameup Effort

On Oct. 6, 1986—less than seven months after the Illinois primary—400 federal, state and county police invaded the offices of the LaRouche-associated Campaigner Publications in Leesburg, Va. FBI and Virginia State Police special sniper units were backed up by a Loudoun

County SWAT Team. Helicopters, fixed-wing aircraft and even an armored personnel carrier were held in reserve at a 4-H fairground a short distance from the farm where Lyndon LaRouche and his wife were staying. In fact, recently disclosed government documents demonstrate Pentagon involvement in the Leesburg raid—specifically the Special Operations unit of the Joint Chiefs of Staff.

The mobilization of an invasion force larger than that used in Grenada in September 1983 to serve two search warrants and four arrest warrants, was not the result of over-zealous planning. Since no later than 1982, Irwin Suall, Mira Lansky Boland (the Jonathan Jay Pollard-linked CIA agent-turned ADL dirty trickster) and an army of other ADL agents and assets had been engaged in a systematic campaign to sic the government on LaRouche. By the time the raid took place, the govermnent raiding party had been so jacked up by ADL disinformation that they were expecting to run into a terrorist armed camp that would make the Irish Republican Army green with envy.

The March 1986 Illinois upset victory provided the ADL and its collaborators in what became known as the Get LaRouche Strike Force with the opportunity and motive to go all-out.

How did it work?

Since the spring of 1982, according to the ADL's own published accounts, Suall and company were closely collaborating with Henry Kissinger, the former U.S. secretary of state, and longtime LaRouche hater. In August 1982, Kissinger wrote to then-FBI Director William Webster the first of a series of personal letters demanding that the FBI move to shut down the LaRouche political movement. In a subsequent, more detailed note in November, Kissinger's attorney lied that LaRouche had foreign intelligence ties—a lie calculated to activate government "active measures" under the guidelines of Executive Order 12333. E.O. 12333, signed by President Ronald Reagan in December 1981, gave the CIA, the FBI and the Pentagon intelligence services broad latitude to investigate and disrupt groups suspected of working for hostile foreign governments.

In January 1983, Kissinger's allies on the President's Foreign Intelligence Advisory Board (PFIAB) made a formal request for such an active measures campaign against LaRouche. The FBI, operating through Judge Webster and Oliver "Buck" Revell, quickly launched such an effort.

Ironically, as the Kissinger-ADL wing of the national security and law enforcement apparatus of the federal government was activating its illegal war against LaRouche, President Reagan—with the backing of his national security adviser Judge William Clark, Defense Secretary Caspar Weinberger and other senior military and security advisers—was moving ahead with the Strategic Defense Initiative, a plan based on a concept advanced by LaRouche even before the Reagan administration came into office. According to court testimony in Roanoke, Va. by Richard Morris, Judge Clark's NSC security chief, LaRouche had worked with the Reagan White House on at least eight national security projects—including SDI—most of which are still classified to this day.

Was this a case of the right hand not knowing what the left hand was doing? Hardly! The ADL and Kissinger were painfully aware of LaRouche's growing influence within the Reagan administration, and they were out to break the rules to shut down all the LaRouche-Reagan ties.

According to court testimony by the ADL's Mira Lansky Boland on May 24, 1990 in Roanoke, Va., she was an active participant from day one in the illegal government covert operation against LaRouche that led to the October 1986 raid, and a series of federal and state criminal prosecutions in Boston; New York City; Alexandria, Leesburg and Roanoke, Va.; and Los Angeles.

The black propaganda aspect of that covert operation which we picked up in Stockholm at the beginning of this chapter was launched at an April 1983 meeting at the New York City office of Wall Street broker and self-styled intelligence agent John Train. Mira Lansky Boland was present at that secret meeting, representing the ADL. National Security Council consultant Roy Godson, a longtime ally of the ADL, was also present, along with a dozen journalists and editors from such organizations as NBC News, *Reader's Digest, The New Republic* and *Business Week.* A CIA funding conduit deeply involved in the secret Iran-Contra operations, the Smith Richardson Foundation, provided the cash for the orchestrated smear campaign against LaRouche.

While much of the anti-LaRouche propaganda spewed out of NBC, *The New Republic,* the *Wall Street Journal* and *Reader's Digest* consisted of name-calling aimed at scaring off active and prospective LaRouche supporters, enough charges of "terrorism" and "international espionage" were thrown in to assure that federal and state prosecutors would be forced to maintain open investigative files and, eventually, to launch grand jury probes.

The "kill phase" of the ADL-led dirty war against

LaRouche was already well underway when the spring 1986 events in Illinois took place.

Financial Warfare

The ADL-John Train black propaganda campaign was not merely aimed at discouraging voters from pulling the levers for LaRouche candidates on election day.

To successfully throw LaRouche in jail—or worse— the ADL set out to bankrupt the LaRouche publishing operations and turn some of LaRouche's own supporters and financial backers against him.

Spending millions of dollars, and working with groups like the CIA-spawned Cult Awareness Network (CAN), ADL dirty tricksters targeted thousands of LaRouche campaign contributors, whose names, addresses and phone numbers were maintained in public files at the FEC. The ADL-CAN operators would contact relatives, financial advisers and friends of the LaRouche supporters, and literally subject them to scare-tactic behavior modification. The techniques used were often those developed in the secret laboratories of the CIA and the FBI for use against enemy prisoners of war and captured spies. Through these highly illegal actions, the ADL built up a profile list of weak and vulnerable people, many senior citizens, whose only "crime" was that they financially supported the legitimate political campaign activities of Lyndon LaRouche. The names of these targets were passed on to the Department of Justice's Get LaRouche Strike Force in a fashion reminiscent of the worst of the Nazi Gestapo operations.

In May 1988, after 92 days of trial, the first federal prosecution of Lyndon LaRouche and a half-dozen of his associates came to a screeching halt when Boston District Court Judge Robert Keeton declared a mistrial. Evidence of wild government misconduct—implicating Oliver North and Vice President George Bush—had disrupted the trial, so that the government wanted to be done with it. As press reports later showed, it had also convinced the jury that any criminal activity associated with the case had been committed by the government, not by Lyndon LaRouche. Prosecution claims of credit card fraud by LaRouche campaign fundraisers and publications salesmen had been thoroughly discredited.

The collapse of the first government effort at framing up Lyndon LaRouche was a direct blow to the ADL. Mira Lansky Boland and Boston ADL official Sally Greenberg had been virtually integrated into the prosecution staff of Assistant U.S. Attorneys John Markham and Mark Rasch.

Although suffering a bad setback in Boston, the ADL-driven prosecution strike force had already opened up a second front in its illegal drive to wipe out the LaRouche movement.

In April 1987, Loudoun County, Va. Deputy Sheriff Don Moore, a Vietnam War Marine bunkmate of Ollie North and a secret paid agent of the ADL-CAN, wrote a patently false affidavit for federal prosecutors, claiming that LaRouche and company were getting ready to pick up stakes and go underground to avoid the pending federal prosecution and the prospect of paying large fines. The Moore affidavit was then used by then-U.S. Attorney Henry Hudson to induce a federal bankruptcy judge to order an involuntary bankruptcy against three LaRouche-identified companies, including two publications with a combined circulation of 250,000 readers. In a highly illegal "hearing" at which no stenographic records were made and where no attorneys representing the three entities were present, the judge was convinced to sign the seizure order. The next day, U.S. Marshals padlocked and seized the same offices that had been raided six months earlier.

Three years later, the same federal bankruptcy court judge, after a full trial of the bankrupty action, reversed his initial ruling and threw out the involuntary bankruptcy, ruling that the government had filed the petitions in "bad faith" and had committed "fraud upon the court." A higher court upheld that ruling, and the government chose not to appeal.

Why appeal it? The damage had already been done!

With the bankrupting of the LaRouche companies, federal prosecutors and FBI agents stepped in to advise thousands of LaRouche supporters that millions of dollars in loans they had made to those companies would not be paid—unless they cooperated with the government railroad of LaRouche.

The claim that money would be paid back if the "victims" played ball with the government prosecutors was another Big Lie. Once the printing presses were shut down, and the publications discontinued under the government trustees, the companies were penniless. No money could be paid back—because the government had taken the viable, successful publishing operations and driven them into the ground: first, through intensive ADL propaganda branding LaRouche a monster, and next through the fraudulent bankruptcy proceeding itself.

In the majority of cases, the LaRouche supporters knew it was the government, not LaRouche, that was behind the bankruptcy and their personal losses. The former supporters who did succumb to the government pressure tactics were invariably those whose families, bankers, friends, etc. were already sucked in by the ADL-CAN dirty war.

Government prosecutors admitted under oath that Mira Lansky Boland of the ADL had served as the "clearinghouse" for trial witnesses in all of the federal and state prosecutions of LaRouche and his associates. Lansky Boland worked from the outset with Don Moore, the Loudoun deputy sheriff who authored and signed the fraudulent bankruptcy affidavit. In September 1992, Don Moore was arrested by the FBI for his role in a plot to kidnap two LaRouche supporters. Moore was working for the ADL-allied Cult Awareness Network in the kidnapping scheme. That case is scheduled to go to trial at the end of 1992.

When in December 1988, a federal jury in Alexandria, Va. convicted LaRouche and six associates on conspiracy fraud charges stemming from the government and ADL-instigated bankruptcies, Mira Lansky Boland was the only non-government official to attend the "victory party" at the prosecutors' office. The conviction had been won on the basis of a pretrial order by Judge Albert V. Bryan, Jr. forbidding defense attorneys from informing the jury that the government had been responsible for the bankruptcy. Back in 1987, Bryan had been the judge who initially upheld that bankruptcy action. At the sentencing of LaRouche and the others in January 1989, Judge Bryan boasted that Boston trial Judge Robert Keeton "owed him a cigar" for ensuring that LaRouche and the others were so quickly convicted and shipped off to prison.

The jailing of LaRouche in what amounted to a thoroughly unjust life sentence did not end the ADL drive to destroy LaRouche and his political movement. The state of Virginia, as part of the ADL's Get LaRouche dirty war, had joined in the feeding frenzy by indicting over 20 LaRouche associates on state charges stemming from the identical bankruptcy scheme.

In a series of trials in Roanoke, Va., the ADL was caught red-handed in a judge buying effort. State Judge Clifford Weckstein, a political protégé of Virginia ADL chief Murray Janus and other top state ADL figures, was provided with a full collection of ADL smear sheets on LaRouche by the League. In a series of back and forth letters released by Weckstein in the trial of one of the LaRouche defendants, it was revealed that Janus and other local ADL officials had mooted they would back Weckstein for a seat on the Virginia State Supreme Court. The implication that his handling of the LaRouche prosecutions would be crucial to his future career on the bench was apparently not lost on the judge. Michael Billington, a LaRouche associate who had already served over two years in federal prison as the result of the Alexandria federal case, was sentenced by Weckstein to 77 years in state prison on patently phony loan fraud charges.

Vandalism in a Mt. Airy, Md. cemetery may have been the work of a satanic cult.

8 The ADL Peddles the New Age

In the summer of 1989, the entire world was reeling in shock and horror over the discovery of a satanic burial ground on a ranch in Matamoros, Mexico. Dozens of mutilated, cannibalized corpses were discovered.

The grisly details of the kidnapping and human sacrifice of one of the cult's victims, Texas college student Mark Kilroy, prompted Texas state legislators to draft a law stiffening the penalties for satanic ritualistic crimes, and making it a criminal offense to conduct certain occult rituals. The governor of Texas convened a special session of the legislature to get the bill passed.

The ADL, while peddling bills all across the country that would make it a crime to *think* anti-Semitic thoughts, launched an all-out effort to defeat the Texas crackdown on satanic crimes, branding the bill "anti-Semitic"! In its jaded logic, the ADL claimed that, technically, the bill made it illegal for rabbis to perform circumcisions on infants. The vast majority of the Jewish community in Texas, including many leading rabbis, refused to buy into the ADL's twisted interpretation, and supported the bill.

Some people began to smell a rat. And they were right.

Not only has the League been an integral part of the organized crime structure that has wrecked America's youth through the peddling of drugs; but as a pivotal institution within the Scottish Rite Freemasonry Southern Jurisdiction, the ADL has been a part of the century-old effort to paganize America under a variety of labels: "secular humanism," "new religions," and, most recently, "the New Age."

Not surprisingly, as investigators probed the higher levels of the "New Age" plot, they found that the New York City Cathedral of St. John the Divine, the headquarters of ADL patrons Bishop Paul Moore and Canon Edward West, was at the very center of the paganization effort. While nominally part of the Anglican-Protestant Episcopal persuasion, the Cathedral was actually the underground headquarters of the Luciferian movement in America.

Killing the Judeo-Christian Tradition

Since 1948, the ADL has devoted over one-third of its legal efforts to support activity that may rightfully be called "the plot to kill God." The ADL has filed dozens of *amicus curiae* (friend of the court) briefs in legal cases often settled by the U.S. Supreme Court, whose results have included banning school prayer, banning released time for religious instruction, banning Christmas carols and spirituals, banning celebration of Judeo-Christian holidays, and most recently banning the Bible as unfit for the classroom; causing federal, state, and local governments to be "neutral" on religious issues, as well as compelling them to cease participation in any display of art associated with the Christian religion, whether during a religious holiday season or other time; and banning prayers in courtrooms, together with religious oaths for courts and government officials.

While the ADL has concentrated upon uprooting the traditions of Western Christian civilization from public life—e.g. by throwing Christianity out the front door of schools—it has not protested as "New Age religion" has been ushered in the back door, now to permeate society. In fact, while condemning any manifestation of Christianity at every turn, the ADL has used First Amendment arguments in court and elsewhere to defend witchcraft and peyote (an hallucinogen derived from a type of cactus) cults.

The ADL has not acted alone in this drive to "paganize" America. It has enjoyed the assistance of some friends in very high places, including the highest court in the land. It began in earnest on Feb. 10, 1947, when Supreme Court Justice Hugo Black rendered the majority opinion in the case of *Everson v. Board of Education.* Black, who was a lifelong member of the Ku Klux Klan and 33rd-Degree member of the Southern Jurisdiction of Scottish Rite Freemasonry, enshrined the following phrase: "In the words of Jefferson, the clause against establishment of religion by law was intended to erect 'a wall of separation between Church and State.' "

During the period of time when the attention of the Court seemed to focus on religion-clause cases, roughly 1949-56, seven members of the Craft served on the Court along with a former Mason, Justice Sherman Minton. Masons continued to dominate the Court, while most of the decisions to uproot Christianity were made, until 1971. The Southern Jurisdiction of Scottish Rite Freemasonry, to which the preponderance of Supreme Court justices belonged from the period of 1939 to 1971, is the self-described "New Age" Jurisdiction.

As Paul A. Fisher aptly demonstrates in his book *Behind the Lodge Door,* the original intent of the religious establishment clause by the Founding Fathers, who shaped this constitutional instrument, was to guard against the state's establishing a theocracy of the Roman cult variety that would persecute those practicing the tenets of Western Christian civilization upon which the republic had been founded. Yet, through Justice Black's "wall" decision in *Everson* and hundreds of subsequent federal, state and local rulings, a Manichean religious cult is on the verge of establishing a "New Age" theocracy in the U.S. today.

The Founding Fathers were deeply religious, and whatever problems may have existed in that regard, they believed that each individual had been created in *imago viva Dei,* in the living image of God, with a divine spark of reason, which they expressed in the principle that "all men are created equal under God." The fallacy of the "wall of separation" cult dogma is shown by the Northwest Ordinance, passed in 1787 and readopted in 1789, which provided that "religion, morality, and knowledge being necessary to good government and the happiness of mankind, schools and the means of education shall forever be encouraged." And, in his Farewell Address to the nation in 1796, President George Washington declared that "religion and morality are indispensable supports [for] political prosperity," and warned that we could not expect "that national morality can prevail in the exclusion of religious principle."

Undoubtedly, Justice Hugo Black's masonically dominated Court would have found these sentiments to be unconstitutional.

As Justice Black's son said of him, he was a man who "could not whip himself up to a belief in God or the divinity of Christ, life after death, or Heaven or Hell." When he first ran for the U.S. Senate, public condemnation compelled Black on July 9, 1925 to "retire from the Robert E. Lee Klan No. 1, but he closed his letter of resignation to the Kligrapp [Secretary], 'Yours In the Sacred Unbreakable Bond.' "

Having won election, Black participated in a secret Klan ceremony witnessed by investigative reporter Ray Sprigle on Sept. 2, 1926, where Senator Black was welcomed back to the Klan with a "grand passport" of life membership at the Birmingham, Ala. state Klan meeting. At the ceremony, Black swore never to divulge, even under threat of death, the secrets of the Invisible Empire. And he said, "I swear I will most zealously and valiantly shield and preserve by any and all justifiable means and methods ... white supremacy. ... All to which I have sworn by this oath, I will seal with my blood, be Thou my witness, Almighty God. Amen."

Ironically, although Sprigle's truthful articles were carried in all the major papers, it was the two flagship journals of American liberalism, *The Nation* and *The New Republic*, that chose to believe Black's denials that he was a Klan member in the 1920s, in a scandal that continued after President Franklin Delano Roosevelt appointed Senator Black to the Supreme Court in 1937.

Fortifying the Wall

The ADL has been among the strongest upholders of lifelong Ku Klux Klan member and Mason Justice Hugo Black's "wall of separation" decision, beginning a year after the 1947 *Everson* opinion containing this new language. A history of that involvement can be found in the ADL's pamphlet, *Friend of the Court 1947-1982: To Secure Justice and Fair Treatment for All* by Jill Donnie Snyder and Eric K. Goodman. In the chapter titled "Separation of Church and State" we find the following:

> "Since 1948, ADL has filed *amicus* briefs in practically every major church-state case, consistently arguing for a strict interpretation of the establishment clause. . . . ADL continues to work for a strict separation of church and state, a commitment that dates back to the League's first involvement in an establishment clause dispute: *McCollum v. Board of Education.* . . . In the *Everson* opinion . . . the Court emphasized in strong language the parameters of the establishment clause. . . . ADL stands firmly committed to a strict separation between church and state. The wall of separation must be fortified and strengthened, so that the religious freedom dreamed of by Jefferson and the other founding fathers, may endure now and forever, an example to the world."

Among the actions in which the ADL has been the historic friend of a masonically dominated Court and of KKKer Justice Black's "wall" reinterpretation of the establishment clause are:

1) *Released time.* From the 1948 *McCollum* case

until the present day, the ADL has fought released time from schools, which gives a release for students to participate in religious education.

One of the most recent cases was *Doe v. Human,* which was affirmed when the Supreme Court refused to hear it, and in which the ADL had filed an *amicus* brief. It resulted in the school system of Gravette, Ark. having to end the practice of released time for religious instruction in the schools on a voluntary basis requiring parental approval. In its pamphlet *ADL in the Courts: Litigation Docket 1991,* the ADL states that this storytime program in Gravette "presents at least two inescapable infringements on the establishment clause—impermissible inclusion of religion in the public schools and forbidden state indoctrination of a particular faith."

Paul Dee Human, the superintendent of schools in Gravette, told a reporter for *Executive Intelligence Review,* "By such cases the stage is being set for a one-world religion. Kids are being brainwashed to death by the New Age religions, and it has become harder and harder to take a Christian stand. . . . There is no question but that the real agenda of groups like the ADL is to usher in the New Age. The more the New Age is brought in, the lesser the boundaries on moral action. 'If it's right for you, it's right' is the guideline of the New Age."

2) *Parochial aid.* The question of public aid for parochial schools was the centerpiece of the *Everson* decision written by Justice Hugo Black, and there have been dozens of parochial aid suits since then. For over thirty years, one of the ADL's strongest allies in such cases has been Americans United for Separation of Church and State. According to the managing editor of *The Scottish Rite Journal,* Dr. John W. Boettjer, Sovereign Grand

Commander C. Fred Kleinknecht relied heavily upon the staff of Americans United for Separation of Church and State to write his call to arms in the November 1991 issue defending Jefferson's "wall of separation," which Kleinknecht calls "the cornerstone of the Constitution."

Boettjer is himself a member of the National Advisory Council of Americans United Against Church and State, that has worked closely with the ADL. Another collaborator of Americans United is Gregg Ivers, who wrote the recent ADL call to arms, which parallels that of Supreme Commander Kleinknecht, titled *Lowering The Wall: Religion and the Supreme Court in the 1980s.*

The full import of Justice Black's membership in the Southern Jurisdiction's New Age religious cult emerges in a letter that 33rd-Degree Mason and Grand Prior of the Supreme Council, Scottish Rite, McIlyar H. Lichliter, wrote to Justice Harold Burton, two years after *Everson.* The letter described Lichliter's pilgrimage to the tomb of Jacques De Molay, who had been Grand Master of the Knights Templar. De Molay was condemned as a heretic after Pope Clement V and the French King Phillip le Bel ordered an investigation, which discovered that upon initiation into this crusading order, members were required to spit upon an image of Christ's face. The Templars were shown to be a Manichean cult, practicing a form of the Middle Eastern Baphomet paganism as an initiation into their inner secrets.

After Jacques De Molay was executed in 1314, as 19th-century Scottish Rite Supreme Commander General Albert Pike stated in his book *Morals and Dogma,* renegade Templars traveling to Scotland helped King Bruce found a precursor of the Scottish Rite, which is also part of the ritual of the New Age Southern Jurisdiction, known as the 30th Degree Knight Kadosh, otherwise known as the "Holy Knight," "Knight of the Temple" and "Degree of Revenge."

According to Pike, the Knights Templar were from the very beginning "devoted to . . . opposition to the tiara of Rome and the crown of its Chiefs. . . ." Their object, Pike said, was to acquire influence and wealth, then to "intrigue and at need fight to establish the Johnnite or Gnostic and Kabbalistic dogma."

According to author Paul Fisher, "The former Grand Commander of the Scottish Rite [Pike] also asserted that the secret movers of the French Revolution had sworn upon the tomb of De Molay to overthrow Throne and Altar. Then, when King Louis XVI of France was executed (1793), "half the work was done; thenceforward, the Army of the Temple was to direct all its efforts against the Pope."

The United States' Founding Fathers well knew the seditious nature of the Scottish Rite, which President George Washington, in a letter to Minister G.W. Snyder, denounced for its "diabolical tenets" and for having unleashed "the pernicious principles" of the Jacobin mob during the French Revolution.

3) *Prayer.* These "wall of separation" cases began in the early 1960s, and they continue today. In the interim, the Supreme Court, with the full approval of the ADL, has been involved in banning non-denominational prayer to a monotheistic God, voluntary prayer, and silent prayer in schools, courtrooms, and at other federal, state, and local government functions. In a related case in which the ADL filed an *amicus* brief in 1961, *Torcaso v.*

Watkins, the Supreme Court ruled it unconstitutional for people seeking public office to be required to take an oath that they believe in the existence of God.

In 1963, with *School District of Abington Township v. Schempp,* the Supreme Court agreed with the ADL's *amicus* argument that Bible reading at the start of a school day is unconstitutional. In the recent case of *Kenneth Roberts v. Kathleen Madigan,* as we shall see, the Supreme Court affirmed the decision of the Tenth U.S. Circuit Court of Appeals, that banned the Bible from being in the schoolroom unless a teacher hid it in his desk. In its pamphlet *Friend of the Court,* the ADL argues that it is seeking to keep the government completely out of religion and vice versa, lest the Jewish minority be overwhelmed by a Christian majority:

> "The horrible consequences of an officially sponsored religion can be seen in the Crusades and, in one of the darkest periods in Jewish history, the Spanish Inquisition. . . . ADL works to ensure a strict separation of church and state so as to protect minority religions. . . . Judaism is a central concern for the League."

But the ADL's hostility, rather than being directed against Christianity, is actually directed against the entirety of the Judeo-Christian tradition, demonstrated when the ADL filed *amicus* briefs to ban display of the Ten Commandments in the classroom in cases paralleling the school prayer issue.

Perhaps the most ironic case, given the ADL's claims to represent Jewish interests, was its stand in the 1980 Ten Commandments case, *Stone v. Graham,* where the plaintiffs challenged a Kentucky statute which required the posting of the Ten Commandments in each school classroom. The ADL ended up fighting a small-print statement after the last Commandment which read:

"The secular application of the Ten Commandments is clearly seen in its adoption as the fundamental legal code of Western civilization and the common law of the United States." In November 1980, the ADL agreed with the Supreme Court's decision that this was unconstitutional.

4) *Christmas carols, hymns, spirituals.* Nearly all of these song forms, which are a most efficient prophylactic to protect children from the horrors of the rock-drug-sex counterculture, and are a bridge to classical music, have been all but banned with the agreement of the ADL from public schools.

One recent case, *Florey v. Sioux Falls School District 49-5,* grew out of a 1978 school board policy which allowed the singing of Christmas carols, the performance of religious plays, and the display of religious symbols in Sioux Falls public schools. Although the ADL filed *amicus* briefs at the level of the Eighth U.S. Circuit Court of Appeals and with the Supreme Court, the latter refused to hear the case, thereby affirming the decision of the Appeals Court that such actions were constitutional, much to the dismay of the ADL.

5) *Equal Access Act (EAA).* Another decision that drew cries of alarm from both the ADL and the New Age Southern Jurisdiction that the "wall was being lowered" involved the EAA. In a June 4, 1990 press release, the ADL said: "The Supreme Court decision today upholding the Equal Access Amendment erodes the wall separating church and state." The case, *Board of Education of West-*

side Community Schools v. Mergens, involved the efforts of a student, Bridget C. Mergens, to have equal access to school facilities for a Christian Bible study club.

According to the ADL release, "The Court held that student sponsored religious clubs in public high schools do not violate the establishment clause of the First Amendment." In its *amicus* brief, the ADL argued that the EAA was unconstitutional, since it involves the public schools promoting religious activities impermissible from the standpoint of the cult dogma underlying the "wall of separation" opinion of Justice Hugo Black.

In its 1991 *ADL in the Courts* pamphlet, the ADL describes its *amicus* brief as having argued the following:

> "The brief contended that both the legislative history of the EAA and the language of the statute itself reveal its impermissible religious purpose. The EAA arose following several unsuccessful legislative and constitutional initiatives to promote religion in public schools. When these efforts failed, Congress adopted the free speech analysis from *Widmar v. Vincent* 454 U.S. 263 (1983), characterizing student religious activity as a protected form of free expression."

What particularly disturbed the ADL was that by granting Christian clubs equal access to school facilities, where there was an open forum for the debate of often competing ideas, the Supreme Court in upholding the EAA had somehow given undue emphasis to the free speech clause of the First Amendment over the establishment clause interpretation of Justice Black.

5) *Religious symbols.* As a result of adjudication since the *Everson* decision, it has become unconstitutional for schools and governments to celebrate Christ-

mas or other Christian holidays with the display of such religious symbols as crosses, Nativity scenes, or depictions of Jesus. Instead, what must be substituted are Santa Claus, reindeer, and Christmas trees, which are of a secular nature and tend to substitute the material aspect of gifts, rather than the religious significance of the founding of Christianity, with the birth of Christ.

The ADL has participated in a number of such cases. Among the recent ones described in its 1991 *ADL in the Courts* pamphlet is *Doe v. Small* 934 F. 2d 743 (7th Circuit) 1991: "At issue in this case was the constitutionality of a public park display of numerous large paintings depicting scenes from the life of Jesus Christ."

The ADL wrote an *amicus* brief in this case from Ottawa, Illinois, saying that the local government's assistance to the Jaycees in preparing the annual display, including the use of public land, violated the "wall of separation." Writes the ADL: "The brief contended that the city is not merely acknowledging or celebrating Christmas, but that it is instead supporting Christianity."

Yet, in the case of *American Jewish Congress v. City of Beverly Hills,* Case No. CV 90-6521, when the American Jewish Congress filed suit against the Lubovitchers for erecting a menorah to celebrate Hanukkah on public property, the ADL worked out a compromise whereby the menorah could be displayed along with a large Christmas tree on land that did not face public buildings.

5) *Banning the Bible.* On June 29, 1992, the Supreme Court let stand a ruling in the case of *Kenneth Roberts v. Kathleen Madigan and Adams County School District No. 50,* that the Constitution prohibits an elementary public school teacher from silently reading the

Bible to himself while his students read secular books. The Court declined to review a decision of the Tenth U.S. Circuit Court of Appeals that Kenneth Roberts, a fifth-grade public school teacher teaching in a suburb of Denver, violated the Constitution by reading the Bible to himself during the classroom's "silent reading period."

The Tenth Circuit had ruled that even having the Bible on top of the teacher's desk in view of the students violates the First Amendment, and Roberts had been forced to hide the Bible in his desk after he was admonished by the principal, Kathleen Madigan. The Appeals Court also ruled it unconstitutional for Roberts to include two Christian books, *The Bible in Pictures* and *The Story of Jesus,* in his 240-volume classroom library among such other books as *Tom Sawyer, The Wizard of Oz,* and *Charlotte's Web.* Also in the classroom library were two books that contained discussions of Indian religions and a book on Greek mythology.

The ADL filed an *amicus* brief with the Tenth U.S. Circuit Court of Appeals. To quote *ADL in the Courts:*

> "ADL's brief argued that the district court properly denied the injunctive relief when it determined that Roberts was using his role as a teacher to advance religion in violation of the *Lemon* establishment clause test. ADL argued that the Supreme Court has recognized repeatedly that to impressionable schoolchildren, religious activities in the public schools convey the message of government sponsorship of religion. This is particularly true when a teacher reads from the Bible in front of students."

However, as even the ADL had to acknowledge, "One of the three judges in the Court of Appeals panel dissented, charging that the school was converting the establishment clause into governmental disapproval, disparagement, and hostility toward the Christian religion."

Polymorphous Patrons

The ADL's hostility to the basic Judeo-Christian principles upon which the United States was founded is blatant. Its support for overtly satanic or New Age "alternatives" to Judeo-Christian moral values, while less public, is also clear upon closer observation.

The League's post-Matamoros efforts to sandbag Texas legislation against satanic-related crimes is one case in point. Another case in point is the ADL's involvement in one of the most outrageous instances of child sexual abuse in recent memory.

The scandal began in Omaha, Nebraska but eventually spread to Washington, D.C., implicating officials of the Reagan-Bush White House in after-hours cavorting with male prostitutes. It has been the subject of thousands of pages of news coverage, several criminal trials, and one book, *The Franklin Cover-up: Child Abuse, Satanism and Murder in Nebraska,* by retired Nebraska state senator and decorated Vietnam war hero John DeCamp.

In late 1988, federal regulators moved in and shut the doors of the Franklin Community Federal Credit Union in Omaha. The institution had been looted into bankruptcy by its founder and manager, Larry King. King, a prominent black Republican Party activist, had been sponsored by some of the most powerful people in town, including the publisher of the only statewide daily newspaper in Nebraska, Harold Andersen, and one of the world's wealthiest men, investment broker Warren Buffett.

Following the blowout of Franklin Credit, evidence began to surface that King, along with many of his prestigious local backers, was part of a VIP homosexual cult which regularly tortured and sexually abused area youth in pedophilic orgies. Further investigations linked King to Washington lobbyist and homosexual Craig Spence. When Washington bunco cops busted a male prostitution ring in the summer of 1989, Spence's name showed up all over the company's records as one of its biggest-spending clients. Spence had high-level White House and GOP connections, and on several occasions had toured the President's home after dark in the company of corporate clients and homosexual prostitutes. According to several accounts, King and Spence were business partners in several call-boy services.

Back in Omaha, a mad dash to cover up the pedophile activities was launched by local FBI officials and the Omaha chief of police, Robert Wadman, himself a member of the homosexual cult, according to numerous witness accounts. Ultimately, King was carted off to federal prison on bank fraud charges, and several efforts to get to the bottom of the pedophile ring were short-circuited.

More questions remain unanswered, but one thing is certain: Alan Baer, a local Omaha multi-millionaire and financial backer of the ADL, was personally caught redhanded in pedophile activities. In 1990, Baer was charged with pandering by local police. He pleaded guilty to a lesser charge rather than face a jury trial with all the attendant media coverage. Baer's name came up repeatedly as a major player in the testimony of victim-witnesses to the child abuse.

The Alan and Marcia Baer Foundation was also listed

as a source of money to several charities, including the Girls Club of Omaha, that were apparently victimized by the child abuse ring. The Foundation also donates to the Gay Men's Health Crisis, Inc. in San Francisco, and the People With AIDS Coalition.

In December 1991, Alan Baer put up the money for a full-page advertisement placed by the ADL in several major newspapers. The ad, headlined "Not All Nazis Are Living in South America," was a fundraising pitch for the ADL.

Bad judgment on the part of the ADL? Or merely one more instance of the ADL's showing its true colors? You be the judge.

Zionist lobby members (clockwise from top left) Rep. Sidney Yates (D-Ill.), Sen. Howard Metzenbaum (D-Ohio), and Sen. Richard Shelby (D-Ala.) are just some of the ADL-AIPAC agents in Congress.

9 The Best Government Dope Money Can Buy

In 1974, Richard Nixon went down for the count as the result of the botched Watergate break-in at the Democratic National Committee's headquarters in Washington, D.C. during the 1972 presidential campaign. As reporters, congressional committees and special prosecutors pored over the details of the Watergate scandal, evidence of a pattern of bribery and coverups emerged that ended up contributing to Nixon's resignation even more than the break-in itself.

Since the fall of Nixon, the American political lexicon has been blessed with such Watergate offspring as "Debategate," "Cartergate," "Irangate," "Bushgate," and "Iraqgate." Political corruption scandals have become as American as apple pie.

Yet despite this growing addiction to political

sleaze, the vast majority of Americans are totally oblivi-
ous to the fact that on any given day, the ADL and its
fellow hooligans in what is euphemistically dubbed the
"Zionist lobby" (the "Dope lobby" is a far more appropriate description) commit crimes against the American
electorate that make Watergate seem tame by comparison. Blackmail, extortion and bribery are such routine
tactics of the Zionist lobby that its primary target-victims,
the United States Senate and House of Representatives,
have been turned into political mush, incapable of governing under the best of circumstances, and completely
paralyzed in the face of the current political and economic crises.

While the media had led the charge against congressional incumbents, appealing to a justified "throw the
bums out" sentiment building among the majority of
voters, the sad reality is that unless the power of the
Zionist lobby is cut down to size, any newly elected
Congress will be like lambs walking to the slaughter, and
nothing will change.

Officially, both the ADL and its leading collaborator
in this corrupting of the Congress, the American-Israel
Public Affairs Committee (AIPAC), are forbidden from
engaging in political campaigning due to their tax-exempt status. Both groups have managed to systematically
break the electoral and tax laws with impunity—largely
due to the fact that they have placed fellow travelers in
key posts in the Executive Branch regulatory agencies
that are supposed to monitor the activities of groups
benefiting from the tax exemptions: the Federal Election
Commission (FEC) and the Internal Revenue Service
(IRS).

Spreading Narco-Dollars

A glimpse at how the Zionist lobby has used the power of the narco-dollar to corrupt and control the Congress is contained in a lawsuit filed in federal court in Washington, D.C. on Aug. 10, 1992. The suit, filed by a group of retired U.S. diplomats against the FEC, charges that the agency failed to impose sanctions against AIPAC for functioning as an unregistered political action committee. Even though the General Counsel at the FEC agreed that AIPAC had violated the law, the Commissioners decided in July 1992 not to take any action against the group.

According to the court papers, AIPAC secretly controls at least 27 different political action committees (PACs) (other investigators place the figure at 59), and uses them to funnel enormous amounts of money to candidates for Congress who support AIPAC's political agenda. Under the FEC statutes, strict limits are imposed on how much money can be given to an individual candidate by a single PAC. The purpose of the regulation is to curb the power of special interest groups in the financing of candidates. By running dozens of PACs, AIPAC, according to the suit, illegally circumvents the law.

The case of the Joint Action Committee for Political Affairs (JACPAC), one of the 27 PACs named in the suit, underscores the tight relationship between AIPAC, the ADL and the political committees. JACPAC lists among its directors the wives of Thomas Dine and Stuart Eizenstat. Since 1980, Dine has been the executive director of AIPAC. Eizenstat, formerly domestic policy adviser to President Jimmy Carter, is the head of the National Jewish Democratic Council (NJDC), an ADL-dominated organization dedicated to winning control over the Democratic Party and placing as many of its members as possible on the staffs of congressmen, governors and mayors.

And where does all of the money come from to buy up the hundreds of congressional seats currently owned by ADL-AIPAC?

A brief look at the Roundtable PAC, one of the 27 outfits cited in the lawsuit as AIPAC-owned, answers that question. Roundtable PAC was founded in 1981 by a group of leading ADL and AIPAC officials and contributors, led by Malcolm Hohlein, the head of the Jewish Community Relations Council of New York. From day one, it was housed in the Manhattan offices of a tax shelter firm called Integrated Resources. Integrated was a thinly veiled money conduit for Michael Milken and his crew of junk bond peddlers and dope money washers at Drexel Burnham. In fact, Drexel CEO Stephen Weinroth, the liaison between Milken and Ivan Boesky in their insider trading scams, was a director of Integrated. All of Milken's prime "investors" socked their money into Integrated as a tax dodge. All of them also poured contributions into the Roundtable PAC.

Among the biggest donors to Roundtable: Ivan Boesky, Robert Davidow (Milken's personal aide at the Beverly Hills office of Drexel), and the sons and daughters of Meshulam Riklis, Laurence Tisch, Saul Steinberg and Paul Milstein (of Carl Lindner's United Brands).

When the Roundtable PAC holds its meetings, guests of honor include, respectively, New York and Minnesota Attorneys General Robert Abrams and "Skip" Humphrey, and N.Y. Sen. Daniel Patrick Moynihan. All are regular recipients of AIPAC PAC dollars. In return for such generosity, Senator Moynihan in 1986 shepherded a tax code revision through the U.S. Congress that gave Integrated Resources an added $43 million in tax breaks. With friends like Moynihan in key posts in the U.S. Senate, Integrated could afford to be generous—at least for a while.

The relationship between Milken and Integrated was so tight that within three months of Milken's indictment in March 1989 for insider trading, Integrated defaulted on $1 billion in short-term loans. It seems that without the running pipeline of hot money from Milken's bottomless Caribbean cash pool, Integrated was lost.

The AIPAC-ADL-run political action committees, in short, represent the combined financial clout of the Lansky dope syndicate! Any similarity between ADL-AIPAC and the genuine national interests of the state of Israel or the Jewish people is purely coincidental.

All told, 211 candidates for the U.S. House and Senate from 48 states received money from the ADL-AIPAC PACs between Jan. 1, 1991 and March 31, 1992. Of the 211 recipients, 187 were incumbents. The total amount given in that 15-month period was well over $2 million, making ADL-AIPAC the second largest source of institutional money to candidates for federal office, second only to the combined donations of all of the labor union PACs. By October 1992, that figure had soared past the $3 million mark.

The ADL-AIPAC PACs don't funnel the majority of their money into Jewish candidates, or even into candidates running for office in states where there are large Jewish populations. More typical of the kinds of office-holders and candidates who receive AIPAC payoffs is Richard C. Shelby, a first-term Democratic U.S. senator from Alabama who has recently gained notoriety for pushing a death penalty bill for the District of Columbia. Shelby received $67,800 from the AIPAC PACs in the 15 months beginning in January 1991, with a career total of $133,825.

Another record-setting recipient of AIPAC largess is Sen. Tom Harkin, the Iowa Democrat who ran an unsuccessful bid for the Democratic presidential nomination in 1992. Harkin came into the Senate in 1984 by defeating incumbent Roger Jepsen, who in 1981 had cast a decisive vote against AIPAC in a fight over the sale of AWACS surveillance aircraft to Saudi Arabia. In his first Senate bid, Harkin received over $100,000 from the AIPAC combine. His career total in AIPAC money is a staggering $366,130!

A total of 29 current incumbent senators and congressmen have received over $100,000 in illegal contributions from the ADL-AIPAC PACs. A dozen have received $50,000 or more just for their 1992 re-election campaigns.

That "dirty dozen" are: Richard Shelby (D-AL), Mel Levine (D-CA), Timothy Wirth (D-CO), Daniel Inouye (D-HA), Barbara Mikulski (D-MD), Christopher Bond (R-MO), Kent Conrad (D-ND), Robert Packwood (R-OR), Arlen Specter (R-PA), Harris Wofford (D-PA), Thomas Daschle (D-SD), and Robert Kasten (R-WI).

Plumbers Unit

Narco-dollars are the key to the ADL's hold over the U.S. Congress, but the League and its AIPAC associates have other trump cards as well. Both groups operate secret, highly illegal spy units that gather blackmail material and carry out dirty tricks against political opponents.

When Richard Nixon got caught running such a

"plumbers unit" at the offices of the Committee to Re-Elect the President (CREEP) in 1972, the American people demanded his scalp. It remains to be seen what the reaction will be now that AIPAC has had its first damaging defection—from its own "plumbers unit."

Gregory Slabodkin worked for a number of years in AIPAC's Policy Analysis unit. Slabodkin eventually got turned off by some of the dirty deeds he was ordered to carry out by the unit's chief, Michael Lewis, and he quit his job and went public with his story. Not surprisingly, Michael Lewis is the son of Dr. Bernard Lewis, the Oxford-trained Arabist who was the architect of the Carter administration's "Arc of Crisis" policy which abetted Ayatollah Khomeini's Islamic Revolution in Iran and the spread of fundamentalism throughout the region.

Policy Analysis, the super-euphemistic name given to AIPAC's "plumbers," maintains dossiers on thousands of American activists—many of them Jewish! University professors who criticize AIPAC or ADL's activities are placed on a blacklist. Their lectures are monitored by spies, who occasionally stage noisy disruptions. Their homes and cars are vandalized. University alumni linked to ADL and AIPAC threaten to pull financial backing from the schools unless the targeted faculty members are immediately fired or blocked from tenure.

Members of Congress are cast as either friends or targets of the ADL-AIPAC syndicate. If they are on the friendlies list, they may be the recipients of weekly computerized blackmail dossiers on some of their colleagues and other policy shapers, which are called "Activities." The "Activities" dossiers are sent out in plain white envelopes bearing no organizational emblems. Deniability is a priority, and the whole filthy blackmail and extortion program was 100 percent deniable—until Slabodkin's defection—complete with reams of AIPAC documents.

AIPAC's unit maintains a singularly close link to the ADL's parallel Fact Finding department, which engages in the exact same kind of activity. In fact, shortly after Thomas Dine took over as executive director of AIPAC, he hired Amy Goott as the first full-time staffer of the Policy Analysis unit. Goott had worked for years at the ADL; her shift of address was apparently blessed by her bosses at the League, and she continued for a period of time to work for both agencies, thereby assuring near-total integration at the covert operations level.

One feature of the job that ultimately got under Gregory Slabodkin's skin was the fact that many of his targets were themselves prominent Jewish activists, usually affiliated with left-wing causes in both the United States and Israel. Many were outspoken critics of the Israeli Likud government's brutality toward the Palestinians living in the occupied territories. Many simply favored a peaceful and equitable solution to the Arab-Israeli conflict. Many of these Jewish activists were treated to the same violence and vicious smearing by ADL-AIPAC that was meted out to Palestine Liberation Organization (PLO) officials!

This "McCarthyite" targeting of prominent Jews who simply bucked the ADL or AIPAC on some policy issue or financial deal underscores the fact that the League and AIPAC are anything but a Jewish "defense organization."

What You Can Do

It should be clear by now that the ADL is one of the most pernicious agencies working to destroy the United States, through the subversion of law and moral values, through the peddling of illegal drugs, through the blackmailing and extortion against Congress, through the looting and trashing of our industrial and manufacturing base, and through its collusion with hostile foreign agencies. Volumes could be written cataloguing the century of treachery by the ADL and its "mother lodge," the Order of B'nai B'rith.

But now is not the time to dwell on details. Now is the time to do something. The ADL continues to thrive as long as Americans remain passive in the face of this subversion. The ADL is not "out there." It is alive and well right in your own backyard.

Although it maintains its national headquarters at 823 United Nations Plaza in New York City (sharing space with the Trilateral Commission), the ADL now has offices in 31 cities across the United States. The ADL has divided the entire country into regions, so that even those cities and states where the ADL does not maintain full-time offices are targeted by their subversive activity.

What kinds of things does the ADL do that immediately affect your life and the lives of your children and neighbors?

They have infiltrated your local police. It stands to reason that an organization as deeply tied to the international dope trade as the ADL would place special priority on getting inside the local police to undermine the police's efforts.

This they have done with a vengeance.

Since the early 1980s, the ADL has sponsored a half-dozen junkets to Israel for local police chiefs, sheriffs and public safety directors. By now, every ranking big city and big county law enforcement executive—with rare exceptions—has enjoyed the ADL's all expenses paid tours of Israel. The top cops are wined and dined, and given the hard sell by the Israeli Mossad, Israeli Defense Force and National Police. The Israeli government's brutal treatment of the Palestinian residents of the occupied territories is held up as the model of how to deal with protesters and demonstrators.

Beginning in 1982, the ADL launched an ambitious drive to have every state in the Union pass a "hate crime" law modeled on the League's own draft legislation. The bills all add longer prison sentences and steeper fines in cases where a crime victim was targeted because of his or her race, religion or nationality. Although prejudice is an evil that must be overcome, the ADL bills, which are now on the books in all but four states, create a category of Orwellian "thought crimes" in flagrant violation of the United States Constitution.

Recently, the U.S. Supreme Court and the state supreme courts in Wisconsin and Ohio have struck down versions of the ADL "hate crime" bill as violations of the First, Fifth, and Sixth Amendments.

Despite these recent reversals, the ADL has managed to parlay the hate crime push into even deeper infiltration and subversion of law enforcement. Through its assets in the U.S. Congress, the ADL pushed through a string of federal laws requiring the U.S. attorney general to prepare an annual report on incidents of hate crime. Having cornered the market in monitoring so-called hate crimes, the ADL was able to insinuate its regional officers into police training seminars, practically writing the curricula and drafting all the textbooks and training aides.

Not only has the ADL made millions of dollars peddling this Orwellian "hate crime" racket. It has also used the infiltration of law enforcement to spread its own brand of hatred: Blacks are inherently anti-Semitic; Arabs, including Arab-Americans, are sub-human; anyone opposed to the Zionist lobby is automatically suspect as a left radical or right radical anti-Semitic terrorist.

As citizens and taxpayers, you have the right to know whether your local police have been subjected to brainwashing by the ADL. Ask your police chief or sheriff whether he has been on one of the ADL junkets, or whether his department has received ADL "training." If the answer is "yes," demand to see the training manuals. Find out whether the ADL is "helping" your local police or sheriffs in maintaining their informants—by either financing those programs or even running them. As far-fetched as this may seem, especially given what you now know about the ADL's ties to organized crime, there are local police departments around the country that have brought the ADL into their most sensitive intelligence gathering, usually out of naivete and desperation over shrinking budgets.

Most states today have freedom of information laws that require police agencies to publicly release documents—including documents about ties to private agencies like the ADL.

Subverting Your Schools

They are subverting your children's education. Complementing their highly successful infiltration and subversion of your local police and sheriffs departments, the gangsters and social engineers over at the ADL have conducted an equally pernicious assault into your school system, using some of the most sophisticated New Age techniques.

Under the rubric of their "A World of Difference" program, ADL officials have succeeded in "training" tens of thousands of public school teachers and administrators to "combat prejudice." In fact, teachers all over the country who have been exposed to the ADL "prejudice" curriculum have complained bitterly that the film strips, training volumes and other slick multi-media tools peddled by the League actually teach prejudice—against African-Americans, Arabs, Catholics and others.

Despite these occasionally surfaced protests, the ADL has managed to penetrate deep into the school system, in part due to the assistance of the National Education Association (NEA), one of the nation's largest teachers unions and a longtime peddler of New Age values and curricula.

The "A World of Difference" program, which got its start in 1986, is now operating in 26 of the 31 regional ADL offices. Concretely, this means that chances are very good that your children and their teachers have been exposed to this ADL subversive propaganda. Through its ties to the Hollywood entertainment industry, dating back to the gangster era of Prohibition, the ADL frequently attracts well-known Hollywood celebrities to participate in their classroom videos, thus adding to the aura of respectability.

What the ADL avoids mentioning is the fact that the money to launch "A World of Difference" came from Hollywood's own junk bond king and inside trader, Michael Milken. Milken personally ripped off billions of dollars from the U.S. economy during the 1980s, and in appreciation for the ADL's role in covering up his crimes, he passed millions of dollars into their hands. One of those million-dollar tax writeoffs went to launching "A World of Difference."

Just as you have a right to know whether your local police and sheriffs have been subjected to ADL "training," you are entitled to know whether the public schools financed by your tax dollars are ruining your children with ADL propaganda. The next time you attend a PTA meeting or speak with your children's teachers or the school principal, ask about the "A World of Difference" program. Is it being used in your children's school?

Ask your local board of education whether they have purchased audio-visual teaching material from the ADL or whether they have budgeted to send teachers

through one of the ADL's frequent "A World of Difference" seminars. Tens of thousands of teachers from coast
to coast have been subjected to this New Age program-
ming over the last six years. Call up the ADL or write to
them at 823 United Nations Plaza, New York, N.Y. 10017
to get a copy of their catalogue, "Human Relations Materials for the School." Read it for yourself and get an idea
of the kinds of prejudices and fears being peddled on
your children.

Demand that these programs be shut down, now!

The easiest thing for you, the citizen, to do, is to act
to prevent the ADL from continuing to use a tax-exempt,
"public interest" cover for its political activities, and
worse. The ADL is supposed to be prohibited by its
501c(3) status from political action, but it violates the
rules every day. Call your congressman or the Internal
Revenue Service to file a complaint. The IRS can be
reached at 1-800-829-1040.

And, last but not least, make sure that your neighbors and friends are made aware of the dangers represented by the ADL presence in your community. Pass
this book around, talk it up among your friends and
colleagues. The prospects of retaking the country are
dim until the influence of the Anti-Defamation League is
erased!

You can order additional copies of this book from:
Ben Franklin Booksellers, 107 South King Street, Leesburg, Va., 22075. Phone 1-800-453-4108. Fax: 1-703-
777-8287. The cost is $7 plus $3.50 shipping and handling for the first copy and $.50 shipping and handling
for additional copies. Virginia residents please add 4.5%
sales tax. Visa and MasterCard accepted.

Chapter Notes

Chapter 1   150 Years of Perfidy

Much of the material for this chapter comes from B'nai B'rith sources, including Edward E. Grusd's semi-official history of the Order of B'nai B'rith, *The Story of a Covenant* (New York: Appleton-Century, 1966); and Esther L. Panitz's biography *Simon Wolf—Private Conscience and Public Image* (Madison, N.J.: Fairleigh Dickinson University Press, 1987). For the history of the U.S. Secret Service during the Civil War period, see LaFayette C. Baker's autobiography and his one-volume history of the Secret Service.

There are also a number of recently published biographies of Judah P. Benjamin and August Belmont from which the information about these two seminal B'nai B'rith collaborators was derived. Particularly useful was David Black's *The King of Fifth Avenue—The Fortunes of August Belmont* (New York: The Dial Press, 1981). See also *The New Federalist* newspaper, September-November 1992, for a series of articles by Anton

Chaitkin which detail the role of General Albert Pike and the Scottish Rite Southern Jurisdiction of Freemasonry in the Confederate secessionist insurrection and in the later founding of the Ku Klux Klan.

Henry C. Carey's treatment of the British Opium Wars against China and India is found in his 1853 work *The Slave Trade, Domestic and Foreign.* The complete series of American System of Political Economy works is published in reprint by the Augustus Kelly Publishing House of Philadelphia. The authors also drew heavily on a series of articles by Paul Goldstein and Mark Burdman which appeared in the December 1978 issue of *The Campaigner* magazine.

The concluding section of this chapter was based on a series of articles published in the *Washington Post* and the *Washington Times* in the summer of 1992, as well as the ADL's 1992 report *The Anti-Semitism of Black Demagogues and Extremists.*

Chapter 2   A Public Relations Front for Meyer Lansky

For a basic biographical profile of Morris Dalitz, including his lifelong collaboration with Meyer Lansky, his role in Hollywood and Las Vegas, etc. see Hank Messick's *Silent Syndicate.* For the material regarding the Bronfman family's involvement in Prohibition-era bootlegging, see *The Bronfman Dynasty: The Rothschilds of the New World* by Peter C. Newman (Toronto: McClelland & Stewart Ltd., 1978). See also *Dope, Inc.,* third edition, (Washington, D.C.: Executive Intelligence Review, 1992), which provides an important overview of the world narcotics trade, including several chapters dealing with the role of the Bronfman family.

There are several biographies of Meyer Lansky from which the authors drew information. By far the most detailed and useful of these is the 1971 book by Hank Messick, *Lansky.* Messick had access to police files and other government records which have been either ignored or not made available to other authors. One recent Lansky biography, *Little Man— Meyer Lansky and the Gangster Life,* by Robert Lacey (Boston:

Little, Brown & Co., 1991) does contain some useful information about the Lansky organization.

For a critical source book on the early history of Jewish organized crime in America and around the world, see Albert Freed's *The Rise and Fall of the Jewish Gangster in America.*

The involvement of Sterling National Bank in the Banca Privata theft is detailed in the files of the United States District Court for the Southern District of New York, case citation *Adolfo Dolmetta, Giovanni Rubboli and Vittorio Coda against Uintah National Corporation, David M. Kennedy, Sterling Bancorp a/k/a Standard Prudential Corporation, Sterling National Bank & Trust Company et al.*

Maxwell Raab's links to Meyer Lansky are reported in Messick's *Lansky.* The details of the Arnold Burns offshore illegal tax shelter scam are contained in a series of news stories in the *Washington Times* by reporter George Archibald, published during the summer of 1988. The links between Dore Schary and Abner Zwillman are from a series of FBI documents obtained through a Freedom of Information Act (FOIA) lawsuit regarding FBI files on the Anti-Defamation League. All told, the FBI has released several thousand pages of material regarding the ADL covering the period from World War II through the early 1980s. Additional files are still being reviewed for public disclosure.

Chapter 3   The ADL and the Opium War
Against America

For details of the Kenneth Bialkin and Willkie, Farr and Gallagher links to Robert Vesco, see United States District Court for the Southern District of New York case citation *Fund of Funds Limited, FOF, Proprietary Funds Limited, IOS Growth Fund Limited against Robert L. Vesco, Norman P. LeBlanc, Milton Meissner, Allen F. Conwill, Bank of New York and Willkie Farr & Gallagher,* 74 CIV 1980 (CES).

Additional information on Meyer Lansky's involvement with Investors Overseas Service (IOS) is found in Hank Messick's *Lansky.* The role of Kid Cann and the Minneapolis branch of the National Crime Syndicate in the Meyer Lansky organization is spelled out in a series of articles appearing in *The New Federalist* newspaper in 1991 and 1992. Other details about the Minneapolis ADL network are found in *Not the Work of One Day*, a six-volume oral history of the ADL published by the League and available at the Library of Congress in Washington, D.C.

For information on Meshulam Riklis' involvement with the Robert Vesco transactions and the Michael Milken junk bond operations, see Connie Bruck's *Predators' Ball: The Inside Story of Drexel Burnham and the Rise of the Junk Bond Raiders* (New York: Simon & Schuster, 1988). A very slanted, albeit detailed version of Edmund Safra's dealings with Kenneth Bialkin and American Express is found in Brian Burroughs' *Vendetta—American Express and the Smearing of Edmund Safra* (New York: Harper Collins, 1992). Burroughs admits that his book is so biased in favor of Safra that he was accused of taking a $1 million payoff from Safra, an allegation he does not explicitly deny. Scores of articles from the *Wall Street Journal* and the *New York Times* also provided critical background information on the Safra-Bialkin-ADL relationship. For details on the role of Arthur Liman, Safra and Bialkin in the Iran-Contra scandal, see the records of the House-Senate Select Panel on Iran-Contra, as well as the hundreds of in-depth news accounts published in all of the major American daily newspapers during 1986-87.

Chapter 4   The ADL and the Junk Bond Bandits Rip Off America

A number of recent books on the junk bond swindles that rocked Wall Street and the investment community during the late 1980s were used in the writing of this chapter. Among the most useful of those books was Connie Bruck's *Predators' Ball*. Also invaluable was James Stewart's *Den of Thieves* (New York: Simon & Schuster, 1991). Stewart, an editor of the *Wall Street Journal*, drew on hundreds of articles published in that newspaper over a several-year period in writing his study. Jesse Kornbluth's *Highly Confident—The Crime and Punishment of Mi-*

chael Milken (New York: William Morrow and Co., 1992) also provided valuable information.

Information pertaining to the various tax-exempt foundations and charitable trusts cited in this chapter came from The Foundation Center, a research library on tax-exempt organizations maintained in New York City and Washington, D.C. by the Russell Sage Foundation.

Chapter 5   Colluding With Terrorists

The text of Judge William Webster's speech was obtained from the Washington, D.C. National Press Club files. Robert I. Friedman's book *Kahane* provided details on the Jewish Defense League's sponsorship by the head of the Brooklyn ADL, the Alex Odeh assassination and some information on Mordechai Levy. A spring 1986 *Executive Intelligence Review* special report, "Moscow's Secret Weapon—Ariel Sharon and the Israeli Mafia," provided additional background information on Mordechai Levy. Numerous stories appearing in the *Philadelphia Daily News* and the *Philadelphia Inquirer* in 1979 were also consulted. The Kathy Ainsworth story drew upon a 1970 *Los Angeles Times* story by its Washington, D.C. bureau chief Jack Nelson.

Chapter 6   In Bed With Communist Dictators and Spies

For a partial account of the Jonathan Jay Pollard affair and the involvement of Kenneth Bialkin, see Wolf Blitzer's semi-authorized biography of Pollard, *Territory of Lies* (New York: Harper & Row, 1991). Additional material on the Pollard affair was gathered from the *Washington Post*, the *Wall Street Journal* and the *Jerusalem Post*.

Edgar Bronfman's involvement with the East German government was detailed in a report issued in 1991 by the Wehrkunde, Western Germany's military studies center in Munich. A prominent law professor and military historian was commissioned to review the captured archives of the East German Foreign Ministry, and the results of his study relating to Edgar

Bronfman and the World Jewish Congress were published in summary news accounts in *Bild Zeitung, Frankfurter Allgemeine Zeitung* and *Semit.*

The Palme assassination material was drawn from Swedish daily newspaper accounts of the murder and the several-year-long investigation.

Information on the U.S. Justice Department's Office of Special Investigations (OSI) was obtained from public files of the Dept. of Justice and from material released under the Freedom of Information Act to relatives of John Demjanjuk. Linda Hunt's *Secret Agenda* (New York: St. Martins Press, 1991) provided some details on the Dr. Arthur Rudolph case.

Chapter 7   Railroad!

All of the information used in this chapter is found in two published source books on the LaRouche trials, both published by the Commission to Investigate Human Rights Violations. *Railroad! U.S.A. vs. Lyndon LaRouche, et al.* (Washington, D.C., 1989) includes extensive documentation from the court records of the Boston and Alexandria trials, as well as a detailed chronology of the frameup. A second 1992 pamphlet contains the full text of LaRouche's 2255 motion for a retrial, which presents new evidence of the government and ADL frameup effort.

Chapter 8   The ADL Peddles the New Age

The ADL's involvement in the effort to defeat Texas legislative initiatives against satanic crime was reported in local newspaper stories in Dallas and Houston, Texas during the summer of 1989.

The biographical information about Justice Hugo Black may be found in Paul A. Fisher's *Behind the Lodge Door: Church, State and Freemasonry in America* (Washington, D.C.: Shield Publishers).

For details on the ADL's legal interventions, see Jill Donnie Snyder and Eric K. Goodman's *Friend of the Court, 1947-1982: To Secure Justice and Fair Treatment for All* (New York: The

Anti-Defamation League of B'nai B'rith). Also see *ADL Law Report: ADL in the Courts—Litigation Docket 1991* (New York: Anti-Defamation League of B'nai B'rith, 1992). Additional material was obtained from the case file of *Kenneth Roberts against Kathleen Madigan and Adams County School District No. 50, Petition for Writ of Certiorari to the United States Court of Appeals for the Tenth Circuit,* in the Supreme Court of the United States, Washington, D.C.

A detailed account of the Omaha, Nebraska pedophile scandal is contained in John DeCamp's important book, *The Franklin Cover-Up—Child Abuse, Satanism and Murder in Nebraska* (Lincoln, Nebr.: ATW, Inc., 1992).

In addition to its role in the Omaha satanism scandal and the effort to prevent anti-satanic legislation in Texas, more recently the ADL has been implicated in a kidnapping plot directed by the Cult Awareness Network (CAN). Nominally a group providing information and counseling to victims of cults, CAN, a longtime ally of the ADL, has been identified in recent court documents as engaging in nationwide kidnapping operations and using aversive behavior modification techniques on their victims. Leading CAN associates were formerly associated with U.S. government secret experimentation with psychedelic drugs under the CIA's MK-Ultra project and other similar programs.

Chapter 9   The Best Government Dope Money Can Buy

The July 1992 issue of *Washington Report on Middle East Affairs* provided a detailed breakdown of the payments made by the ADL and political action committees controlled by the American-Israel Political Affairs Committee. That same magazine published an article by Gregory Slabodkin detailing his activities as an undercover dirty trickster for AIPAC. Robert I. Friedman's two-part series of articles published in *The Village Voice* in August 1992 also provided further details about AIPAC's dirty tricks unit.

For another detailed study of ADL political dirty tricks, see also *Conspiracy Against Freedom; A Documentation of One*

Campaign of the Anti-Defamation League Against Freedom of Speech and Thought in America by the staff of the Liberty Lobby (Washington, D.C.: Liberty Lobby, Inc. 1986). This 228-page report includes court documents and internal ADL memos revealing interference in Federal Communications Commission-regulated broadcasting efforts of a group targetted by the ADL.

Index